THE WILL

A PLAY BY SANDRA SEATON

EAST END PRESS

November 2015 Edition
ISBN: 978-0-9968152-2-2

Note on Musical Selections: Although the selections in the
original production were from Verdi's *Il Trovatore*, the
singer/actress who plays the role of Patti may select arias
or art songs from her own repertoire that are appropriate for
the time period in the play. CD with music and sound
effects is available upon request.

How I Came to Write *The Will*

These notes provide some background information about my play *The Will*. Since childhood, I had heard the story about an ancestor of mine named Israel who sassed a white man and had to be smuggled out of town disguised as a woman. According to the story, when the Ku Klux Klan came to the house looking for Israel, my great-great-grandmother Eliza refused to disclose his whereabouts. Just minutes before, she had hid Israel upstairs under a mattress. After his escape, no one saw or heard from him again.

I had been told often that my great-great grandmother, Eliza Webster, her parents Annie and Demps Cherry, and four others (all free blacks) had founded the first black Baptist Church, Mt. Lebanon, in Tennessee in the 1840's. I also knew that Eliza and her husband Cyrus had had 22 children together, seven of whom died in the smallpox epidemic. That was all I knew. With what resources I had, I had been doing some research (snooping in attics, basements, churches, and talking to people) since 1989. On my trips to Tennessee I went to churches, cemeteries, and courthouses. As a native of Tennessee and through family oral traditions, I knew that an African American free black community existed in middle Tennessee before the Civil War, one with ties to the free black community in New Bedford, Massachusetts.

I was anxious to find out any information I could about Cyrus and Eliza, so I made a trip to the Tennessee State Archives in Nashville. Doing work at archives can be time-consuming and unrewarding; you're lucky if you find anything at all. There wasn't much about African Americans there. Census records revealed that Cyrus had held farmland in Columbia before the Civil War. An 1850 record listed Cyrus, Eliza and a few of their children. Fascinated by the thought of African Americans of that era holding property in the South, and because of my desire to realize a full picture of the world of African Americans, I took a room at a hotel downtown and spent days at the Archives. I think I spent half the time, trying to coax the microfilm readers or rewinding the rolls of film. I followed a number of leads but hadn't turned up much.

On my last day at the State Archives, a very hot summer afternoon about ten minutes before closing, I accidentally found the wills of my great-great grandfather and grandmother, documents that had not been catalogued or listed in the holdings of the Archives. As I read the two wills, I was awe-struck by their evocation of individuals and a way of life entirely different from the stereotypes about African Americans of their place and time. As I read, I was amazed by the beauty of the language and the care evident in each perfectly crafted sentence. My great-great-grandfather Cyrus's will showed great planning and care. He was the nurturer--revealing what we would consider today feminine qualities- -listing things like teapots, mirrors, and blankets; using terms of endearment for each family member--a gentle, loving man. My great-great-grandmother's will, Eliza's, on the other hand, concerned itself with the disposition of the land, down to the last foot.

I was startled to notice that both wills mentioned Israel. Cyrus's will left money and household items to Israel should he return. Eliza's will contained a touching bequeath to Israel pointing any reader of the will away from Israel's actual destination. Archives are even quieter than libraries, but you know when I read those two wills, I couldn't help it; I cried and cried. It was as if after all those years, there they were waiting quietly for me to find them.

I made copies of the wills and returned to Columbia that evening even more determined to find out everything I could about Cyrus, Eliza and Israel. I could still hear my grandmother Emma's words whenever the family drove by Greenwood Cemetery. "When are y'all going over to that cemetery? My grandpa's buried in that cemetery." There was never an answer. Greenwood was the old civil war cemetery. Until the early 20th century, all the white townsfolk, an occasional black servant, and the free blacks who could afford burial there were buried in Greenwood. Not one of my mother's generation, had set foot on the place. When I was younger, I assumed it was indifference; interest often skips a generation. Now I realize that once the Black Codes were firmly in place, my folks no longer felt comfortable going to the white cemetery. New separate cemeteries had been built by that time; to this day, cemeteries in my hometown are segregated.

I desperately wanted to go to Greenwood. I knew there was no way my aunt was going to go with me, so I found a family friend, Mr. Herbert Johnson (His mother, Miss Rebecca, and my grandmother Emma were the end men in the local minstrel shows of their era.), and the two of us put on our old shoes and waded through the grass. Although Mr. Herbert, who was in ill health at that time, needed a cane to get around, nothing could stop this committed history buff from making the trip to Greenwood. We had looked at just about every tombstone we could find when we came to a group over in one corner that faced away from the rest. There they were, my family's graves, just like Grandma Emma had said--Cyrus, Eliza, Eliza's parents, Annie and Dempsey Cherry, seven little graves off in a corner, and next to Cyrus a very large monument with the name Anna Sanders at the top.

The inscriptions were barely readable. I had heard of people doing grave rubbings so we went to a nearby

drycleaner's for some thin paper and to Kmart for crayons.
Back then, grave markers could tell whole stories. After
reading their wills at the archives, it was no surprise that
the tombstones were finely scripted. We rubbed and
rubbed, but were only mildly successful in making out
dates for Cyrus and Eliza. For Anna, I was able to make out
something that I didn't understand, the words "cousin of
Israel Grant." Fresh out of paper, Mr. Herbert and I went to
an auto shop next door. Maybe they had something we
could use. I felt a little uneasy about announcing our
purpose, poking around the white cemetery. A young white
guy at the counter was casual about the whole thing. He
had family over in Greenwood, couldn't help out with
paper, but was on his way home for lunch; he'd bring back
a local historian's book on the cemetery. Just look in the
seat of my pick-up he told me.

Sure enough, an hour later, the car window rolled
down, the book lay there on the seat, waiting. The section
on Cyrus and Eliza listed their inscriptions and the names
of the graves of their seven young children and no more.
There was no information on Anna Sanders. I called the
local historical society. The woman on the phone told me to
go to the grocery store, get some cornstarch or flour, throw
it on the inscriptions, and dust it off. I threw cornstarch on
Cyrus's mother Anna's grave and contemplated the words,
"cousin of Israel Grant;" they just didn't make any sense.
My grandmother had always said we were related to
Ulysses S. Grant. So was Anna the Grant connection? A
light dusting revealed something I never expected to find:
"Anna Sanders, 1790-1852, mother of Cyrus Webster and
consort of Israel Grant." Consort of Israel Grant! Cyrus had
erected a monument over his mother's grave, one of the
largest in the cemetery. And he was proud of his ancestry,
not only proud that a white man was his father, but that his
mother was the common-law wife to this man, a

relationship he cared enough about to inscribe on her tombstone. Here was Cyrus's legacy, the example of a courageous man, courageous enough during slavery, 1852, to announce this relationship to a hostile world, and honest enough to show his love for his father by naming his first born son Israel.

I was fascinated by what I had seen of Cyrus, his eloquent will, his passionate assertion of his biracial identity; all that I knew about him went against stereotype. From that day on, I was fired with the ambition to write a play that would dramatize the people whose characters were expressed in these wills. A play that would be true to them would challenge generally held assumptions about African Americans of their era held by both blacks and whites--assumptions about education, gender roles, and much else. I knew, from family stories, that there were stories that had not been told. Placed in the Civil War era, my characters would reveal a world turned upside down, informed by historical situation and the world of real people, not bound by racial stereotype, but portrayed in their actual circumstances, a way of life entirely different from the stereotypes about African Americans of their place and time. For these past five years, I have been working to bring them to life. Cyrus, the head of the family, whose will is the source of the title, acquired considerable property as a free black before the end of the Civil War. He is determined to pass on not only his worldly possessions but also his spiritual convictions and his wisdom to his descendants. The rebellion of Israel, one of Cyrus's sons, against racial inequities forces Cyrus to act to protect his inheritance in all its dimensions.

Sandra Seaton
July 1989

THE WILL

The Time: July 2, 1866

The Place: Delphi, Tennessee, a small south of Nashville in Maury County. The area has rich agricultural land.

The Set: We see a set with two levels connected by stairs. The lower level, the first floor, is a sitting room. The upper level, the second floor, is divided into two rooms. In the front room on the first floor, there is one black chair in the corner, one teaboard with a black men's hat resting on top. A large kerosene lamp, two other black, ladder-back chairs, a mirror, and two pictures, one of Noah's Ark and the other of George Washington. On the upper level, a feather bed covered with a white bedspread, a large trunk filled with tobacco, two pillows, a pile of bed clothes, hanging on a hook, one small washpot sits on a table beside the bed. A straw hat hangs on the wall. (The lower level is also used for outdoor scenes.)

CAST

CYRUS WEBSTER: father, 58. A mulatto, he is a tall, slender man who moves gracefully but precisely, like a conductor directing a symphony.

ELIZA WEBSTER: mother, 56. Wife of Cyrus. Cherokee and African, dark skinned, thick, heavy hair braided and coiled. A moon-shaped scar on her left cheek that has been there since childhood.

ISRAEL WEBSTER: son, 29. Edgy. Slight build with thick hair that he wears in a Frederick Douglass. He always wears a blue Union jacket.

SIMPSE WEBSTER: son, 24. Tall, slender, he has the same build as his father Cyrus. Poetic, reads Whittier, Longfellow, Lowell.

PATTI BRADSHAW: Simpse's fiancée, 22. Studied music at Roger Williams College in Nashville, she has a lovely soprano voice.

HENRY GARRETT: 49. White man who works for Cyrus Webster. Wears a red scarf around neck.

THOMAS CARL GARRETT: 29. Henry Garrett's son. Wears an old shirt and pants, no hat. Does not wear Confederate uniform.

MAJOR DALEY: A Union man from a well-to-do Tennessee family. White, mature, he is a lawyer and a landowner. He also owns a monument company.

SCENE ONE

[The sitting room of the Webster home in Delphi, Tennessee. Time: July 2, 1866. The Civil War has just ended. In one corner of the room, we see a small shelf filled with books: the Bible, Shakespeare, Tennyson, Emerson. A small portrait of George Washington hangs over the bookcase. In another part of the room, near an oak table and chairs, a writing desk stands under a cluster of dried herbs (asafetida) tacked to a painting of Noah's Ark. Cyrus Webster is writing at a small mahogany desk, cluttered with sheafs of paper, pens, bottles of ink and a small hinged box. Alone in the room, he writes, gets up to pace the floor, then sits down to write again. From time to time, when a door is opened, we hear the conversation of a large family.]

DALEY

[offstage] Cyrus Webster?

>[Cyrus, busy stacking his papers, doesn't pay attention.]

Cyrus Webster? You in there?

CYRUS
>[Cyrus startles, runs to open the door, still carrying a handful of papers, with one hand.]

Major Charles Daley . . . [leads him into room] Major. [As Cyrus smiles, he tilts his head slightly--not a bow, but an African gesture, in deference to the expected kindness of others. The bow can be confused with groveling, but this old world manner is his way of giving respect to anyone he might encounter.]

DALEY

Afternoon. . .

CYRUS

And what do I . . .

DALEY

Should've seen 'em up to the courthouse. Dad-blamed rebs.
Jawin' and carryin on.

**[Cyrus motions to a chessboard on a table. Daley
declines.]**

CYRUS

Tryin' to start it up all over again . . .

DALEY

Can't stand havin' Yanks around.

CYRUS

Rest a spell, Major. **[Cyrus looks at pocket watch
repeatedly. Motions again to the chess board. Daley
declines a second time.]**

DALEY

Not right now, thank you. **[beat]** Dad-blamed rebs. **[beat]**
Drew up the papers. Got 'em right here.   **[Daley holds up
a diagram. Speaks hurriedly.]**   We're lookin' at your
corner of the cemetery.

CYRUS

Just one minute Major.   There.   **[Scribbles on a sheet of
paper, then puts it down hard on desk.]**

DALEY

Over here in your corner.

CYRUS

Right next to my wife's ma and pa. Dempsey Cherry, 1801.

DALEY

Now let's see, your lot...

CYRUS

There, there, she is, those Yanks gon' wonder, a colored aristocrat buried right in the white cemetery.

DALEY

Now don't go startin all that...You got enough left for two more. I 'spect that would be you and Eliza.

CYRUS

Just two? Simpse gettin' married and Israel... That's right-- one of these days, the Websters'll need a whole cemetery, all to themselves.

DALEY

Buy more room.

CYRUS

Major Charles Daley. Selling the stone for a body's last stop

DALEY

Buy more room. That's what you have to do. The folks up at the courthouse, they won't charge you much. Get one of my sons to draw up the papers.

CYRUS

Harvard boys!

[Israel enters, stands off to the side, looks on skeptically. He is wearing a blue Union army jacket.]

DALEY

Never mind about that. Cyrus, your boy Israel needs to watch himself.

[They notice Israel]

ISRAEL

Major Daley's the sheriff, Pa.

DALEY

Magistrate.

ISRAEL

[sarcastically] Keeps us on the straight and narrow. When he's not practicing law and selling lots at the cemetery, he's taking care of all those rowdies around here.

CYRUS

Not much happens around here, Major doesn't know. Don't know how he keeps up with it all.

ISRAEL

Major Daley. Sending all those Daley boys outta town, up to Harvard. Landsakes. And he's the sheriff too!

DALEY

Afternoon, Israel.

ISRAEL

This town's full of Harvard boys.

CYRUS

Harvard boys? Union men! Look at that coat. **[points to Israel's jacket]**

ISRAEL

Afternoon, Major Daley. Pa, you still plannin' to walk the fields before dark?

CYRUS

Not till Simpse brings a little visitor to town. **[to Daley]** Our new addition, the lovely Patti Ann. Things won't be the same around here. Not any more. The girl's traveled. abroad, Major. Sung in I don't know how many towns. **[Cyrus motions toward the chessboard. Daley declines again. Eliza enters.]**

ELIZA

That's all Simpse talks about. Miss Patti and her high society. Been to New York. And everywhere else. We're simple folks. Better not think she can come here, acting all grand.

CYRUS

Now, Mother.

DALEY

Afternoon, Eliza.

ELIZA

Major. **[nods]** If she comes here with her high falutin ways. Expecting to be waited on hand and foot....

CYRUS

Mother, I'm surprised at you.

ISRAEL

Ma's right. Simpse oughta know better.

CYRUS

Give the girl a chance. You hardly know her.

ELIZA

How could Miss High and Mighty look out for a boy like
my Simpse? She'll be treated the same as anybody else,
knocks at our door.

ISRAEL

The opera visits Delphi! Simpse comes marching in with
his sweetheart. **(painful cry)** A little stop on their grand
tour. Come morning, they're gone.

CYRUS

Your brother's settling down. Right here.

**[Eliza picks up an armful of clothes. Looks out
window.]**

ISRAEL

That's right, Pa. Simpse, Major Daley. My brother Simpse,
he's Pa's hope for the future.

CYRUS

Israel Grant Webster, go sit down somewhere. I named
you after my own Pa.

[Israel laughs.]

ELIZA

Hush, Israel. Simpse ought to be here by now. Cyrus?
[exasperated] No point in fixing supper till they get here.

CYRUS

Now, Dolly, they'll be here t'rectly.

ELIZA

Who wants to eat a cold meal? **[leaves room]**

ISRAEL

Ma's still frettin' cause she didn't supervise. Wanted to meet our little songbird at the train herself.

CYRUS

Your ma didn't want any harm to come to the girl, traveling all that way.

ISRAEL

(laughs) Should have gone with Simpse myself. That boy never could get anywhere on time. **[rushes toward door]**

CYRUS

[to Daley. patting Israel on the back.] It's time, Time to start teaching school.

DALEY

Over to Mount Lebanon Church!

ISRAEL

[whirls around] Pa, I just got home.

CYRUS

A day or two a week. Won't hurt you. You'll ease right in.

ISRAEL

On the sly? Like you, Pa? Reading and numbers to the little children. Teach it at the church, so they won't know what you're up to. It's late. Where's Simpse?

CYRUS

Captain Webster, show your schooling. All those bags out
in the barn--mark 'em with our name.

[Israel pauses by the door, then leaves slowly.]

MAJOR DALEY

The finest tobacco in Middle Tennessee. Saw your boy
Israel uptown this morning. Up to the market, acting
strange, real strange. Your boy Israel, the first one up there.

CYRUS

[chuckles] So they tell me. So they tell me. **[beat]** Early
bird.

DALEY

Listen to me, Cyrus. Folks are complainin'. You know how
it used to be, back when we were boys, your folks, they'd
bring their things, buy and trade after the white folks
finished their business. Course, now that everybody's back
from the war...

CYRUS

They're all here, your boys, my boys. Everybody's home.
But they still won't leave it alone.

DALEY

You know Tom Garrett, the one works your land, he started
it, say "You see Israel Webster over there, didn't come late
like the colored used to do, didn't wait till the end of the
morning like they did before. The Webster boy was up
there, musta been the crack of dawn."

CYRUS

Hardly a buyer in sight.

DALEY

No sooner than the words come out of Garrett's mouth--

CYRUS

Fightin' mad since they lost the vote.

DALEY

A bunch of 'em commenced to millin' around. Can't stand the fact our side won. That's why they started up the Klan. Shoulda heard Garrett: "The darkies use to wait till late mornin' to bring their things in, now they come all day, runnin' in 'fore daybreak like a pack of wolves." Pretty soon two colored soldiers came marching by, one watching the other, full turn, forward ho, shoulda seen Garrett and his boys hightail it out of there.

[Henry Garrett and Israel walk back through hauling sacks. They pause and wait for Cyrus to speak. When Cyrus sees Israel, he raises his voice.]

CYRUS

If one of us scares easy, pretty soon they'll run us all off. That's all they need. Might as well all cut and run. If Robert E. Lee couldn't stop me, that crowd sure won't.

DALEY

Robert E. Lee?
[Israel laughs to himself.]
Cyrus Webster, you never fought in the war.

CYRUS

Never you mind whether I went or not. I was fighting before the war. Back in thirty, after we moved into town, I prayed every day, night too, to keep my farming land. I swapped tobacco for horses and plows, put five white men to work and fought off three times that many.

A knock at the door. Eliza descends the stairs slowly then starts towards the door. Cyrus hesitates.]

CYRUS

Watch yourself. I'll get it.

DALEY

Can't be too careful these days.

[Simpse and Patti enter.]
ELIZA

Simpse!

[Eliza runs to Simpse. Patti's face is partially covered with a long scarf. Simpse is carrying a fancy traveling bag and a woman's hat decorated with a large feather. Simpse introduces Patti to Cyrus. Eliza is startled to see Patti.]

PATTI

Miz Webster, Ma'am . . . **[coughs]** All the dust along the road. **[removes her scarf]**

SIMPSE

She has to protect her voice.

[Eliza looks Patti over carefully.]

ISRAEL

Well, I declare.
ELIZA

[to Simpse] I was ready to go along. Thought you'd be more comfortable that way.

SIMPSE

Now, Mother. Everything was fine.

ISRAEL

That's right, Mother. **[extends hand to Patti, then bows.]**
Thought you knew what a gentleman Simpse can be.

[Eliza, mildly irritated, brushes Israel away.]

SIMPSE

Major Daley, Israel--Miss Patti Bradshaw.

[Israel bows.]

DALEY

[tips his hat to Patti and holds it in his hand] Good
evening. And how were things on the road from Nashville?

CYRUS

Folks celebrating?

DALEY

Celebrating? Old glory. When I was a boy, the Fourth of
July--Independence Day--why the best time a boy could
have!

PATTI

[begins to remove her cloak and hat]   I declare I never
heard so much noise—-fireworks, bands of revelers . . .

ELIZA

I see.

SIMPSE

Carrying on, jumping out of the woods.

PATTI

All the way into town.

CYRUS

[to Daley] Her reputation follows her wherever she goes. They say she's every bit the equal of the Black Swan.

DALEY

The Black Swan?

CYRUS

You know the Black Swan? The Black Swan.

DALEY

Oh yes, of course.

SIMPSE

Patti studied singing at Roger Williams.

DALEY

You don't say.

SIMPSE

Yessir--came all the way from Nashville to sing at the Fourth of July picnic.

DALEY

Cyrus, how long you been reciting the Declaration of Independence?

CYRUS

Twenty-three years this July. Day after tomorrow--I'll make it number twenty-four. That's if our sweet nightingale will favor us with a number...

ELIZA

We'll have to look over the program.

CYRUS

Mother, she'll add to the festivities.

PATTI

If it pleases the Websters.

CYRUS

Mother?

ELIZA

We'll see.

CYRUS

If it pleases the Websters? When this young lady finishes her schooling, Lord willing, she'll please our Simpse.

ELIZA

Cyrus!

DALEY

More little Websters.
[Patti turns away, blushing. Eliza hums "Swing low, sweet chariot."]

ELIZA

We ought not be keepin the girl. It's a hard road from here to Nashville. A hard road. **[to Patti]** Let me hear your song for the Fourth.

PATTI

[coughing and adjusting her clothes] Miz Webster, ma'am...

SIMPSE

Ma, she needs to rest. There's only certain times of the day she can …..you know….sing.

CYRUS

We know how to treat guests here.

SIMPSE

It's all the dust, Ma.

ELIZA

Dust never bothered me.[**starts to hum a tune**]

SIMPSE

Ma, she needs to rest her voice.

ELIZA

Just a little song.

SIMPSE

Ma, you don't understand. She needs

ELIZA

To...

DALEY

Pray for good weather, that's what we'll do.

CYRUS

A summer shower christen that lovely gown? Not if we have anything to say about it. [**hugs Patti, then hums "Yankee Doodle"**]

SIMPSE

This way, Patti. I'll show you to your room.

18

ELIZA

[Eliza stops Simpse] Enough of that. Simpse, you set her bag right on the landing.

[Spotlight on Simpse and Eliza together downstairs.]

ELIZA

Well, well, I hear Patti's going around raising money for the school.

SIMPSE

Her voice is as sweet as--

ELIZA

A Christian girl's?

SIMPSE

As sweet as--

[Eliza starts to sing "Swing Low, Sweet Chariot" in a deep, resonant voice.]

SIMPSE

But that's not her idea of singing. She wants to sing, just not...

ELIZA

[Eliza tries to understand, starts to hum again.]
Just not all the time.

SIMPSE

No, she wants to sing a solo.

ELIZA

A solo?

SIMPSE

Oh don't get me wrong. She wants to sing.

ELIZA

[starts to hum "Many Thousands Gone."] Good , we'll
start out with a prayer, then Patti can sing-- "Free at Last"--
that's Mr. Arnell's favorite. After your Pa recites the entire
Declaration of Independence, as he has for the past twenty-
odd years, we'll set out the food. **[starts to sing melody to
"Free At Last"]** After your father's presentation, if he's
not too tired out, he might perform Gray's "Elegy," then
she can sing again.

SIMPSE

Mother, you see Patti, she wants to be appreciated for
herself and for her own contribution to the world of art.

ELIZA

Art?

SIMPSE

Oh Mother! She thinks we can do more than that. You're
not expecting her to sing the way we always do . . . are
you?

ELIZA

And what way is that?

SIMPSE

Ma, you're as bad as the folks at that school. She wanted to
sing Mozart. Had her heart sat on it. Is that a crime? They
were expecting her to sing one of our songs. All those
white folks just waiting for her to sing—---They passed her
this little note with a list of songs. Practiced for weeks. Just

to sing church songs.

ELIZA

You stop talking like that right now, Simpse Webster.

SIMPSE

Now, Ma.

ELIZA

Don't you disrespect the Lord's music. I won't have it. Do you hear me?

SIMPSE

But she's practiced for weeks.

ELIZA

You heard what I said. Simpse... and just where do you think you're going?

SIMPSE

I'm taking Patti's bags to her room.

ELIZA

[Calls to Simpse as he leaves] Your father, he'll be expecting a good Christian song on the Fourth. [goes back downstairs.]

[Divided stage on the second level. Spotlight on Patti upstairs holding up a dress to a mirror and adjusting a hat as Israel watches her from the door. He stands there for a minute then speaks.]

ISRAEL

Is that another disguise or something?

**[Patti, startled, puts things down quickly,
nervously.]**

You know me and my brother, both of us, we're just back
from the war. We have to be real careful. The way you
were all covered up when you came through the door, I was
worried Simpse was bringing home some sort of spy.

PATTI
I've been taught to protect my voice.

ISRAEL
All covered up like that. I can hear them now: who's your
people? They don't take to strangers around here.

PATTI
Me? They say I was born out near Birney Spring. My
mother and the three of us. Didn't stay there long. I've
tried my best to get back here. I've sung in churches,
schools, anywhere along the way. Sunrise service. Helped
set up the benches myself.

ISRAEL
You did, did you? Well, that's good, because Simpse needs
a hard-working wife. Can you run as fast as you can sing?
SIMPSE
[enters suddenly] She's done that too.

ISRAEL
Fourth of July, she might have to sing out in the field. With
ordinary folks.

PATTI
I'll sing anywhere. When we sang at the Opera House in St
Louis, they were right there when we got to the building,
threw all kinds of things, threatened to burn the place

down, I sang anyway. Sang better than I ever had.

[Israel throws his head back in laughter. Patti goes over to Simpse. They stay there together. Israel runs downstairs.]

ISRAEL

Whoa! **[picks up a pan and clangs on it]** Wait'll Tom Garrett hears this! **[to Cyrus]** Perhaps our sweet nightingale will favor us with a selection.

[Cyrus is holding up the cemetery diagram, stops. Eliza crosses to Daley. Patti is upstairs singing scales.]

ELIZA

[to Daley] I thought she was resting her voice. The way these young folks do things these days.

DALEY

Keeps you guessing, alright.

ELIZA

Israel's been back from the war, how long now? Six months, and he's still fretting. Never could get over that yellah gal, Caroline, the one ran off and married that boy from down yonder. Cyrus told you.

[Daley nods, and looks over at Cyrus, who is going over papers on his desk. Patti continues singing scales.]

I don't know what's gotten into that boy.

ISRAEL

[calls out the door and leaves] You all, you all out there, come on in here.

[Henry Garrett enters. Cyrus and Daley pause.]

CYRUS

Henry Garrett.

HENRY GARRETT

Cyrus Webster . . .

CYRUS

The harvest's over, Garrett. You worked our field. You and your boy. Have you marked all your bags?

HENRY GARRETT

Got my bags marked. We got all ours put away.

CYRUS

Then it's the same as before the war. Nothing's changed.

HENRY GARRETT

You think so.

CYRUS

I never left. You didn't either.
HENRY GARRETT
 The boys are back now.

CYRUS

We'll go about our business same as always, Garrett. Set your bags aside, then help us finish bagging ours. That's all there is to it.
[Patti starts to sing an aria upstairs.]

ELIZA

Well, well. I thought she was resting her voice.

SIMPSE

[slightly embarrassed] She's clearing her throat , her chest...

[Israel walks in with Tom Garrett. We can hear Patti singing.]

TOM GARRETT

[yells up the stairs] "Dixie." Sing "Dixie."

[Henry Garrett glares at Tom.]

CYRUS

Tom Garrett, we're done. Me and your Pa, we got things divided up.

TOM GARRETT

Sing "Dixie." The stars and bars.

ISRAEL

Lord have mercy. [to Simpse] He's havin' spells.

CYRUS

Garrett, take your seat over there next to your Pa.

[Simpse and Cyrus are rapt. Israel appears amused.]

TOM GARRETT

Go on, sing.

ISRAEL

Shut up, Garrett. You think you out in the field? He's used to the coon shows.

[Tom Garrett grabs at Israel.]

DALEY

Here, here, that's enough now.

HENRY GARRETT

[to Tom] Boy, sit down. I said, sit down. We're talking business.

[Patti sings a short song in her strongest voice. Tom Garrett mutters something to Israel and runs out. Israel storms out of the room.]

CYRUS

Israel! [beat] Garrett, your boy take care of his bags?

HENRY GARRETT

Like I said, we hauled ours off yesterday. All of it.

CYRUS

That's right. That's right. Now you and the boys, bring our bags in. I want them down in the cellar.

HENRY GARRETT

You better see about your boy, Cyrus Webster.

CYRUS

Never mind about my boy, you and your son, you've got all the tobacco you're going to have. Marked every one of your bags. Everything else is ours.

[Garrett glares at Cyrus, then leaves quickly. Patti finishes her song.]

DALEY

Reminds me of the voice of my dear departed mother.

CYRUS

[eyes Israel as he leaves] Splendid form, splendid. . . . That game of chess won't wait, Major.

DALEY
[returns to sheet of paper] About this tombstone . . .

CYRUS
Ah, yes.

DALEY
Your mother's stone.

CYRUS
Her monument.

DALEY
[reads slowly and carefully] "Anna Sanders, born 1791, died 1866 . . ." Folks are gonna wonder.

CYRUS
That's right--1791 to 1866.

DALEY
Why? They're gonna want to know why?

CYRUS
Why a colored lady, an aristocrat, is buried in the white cemetery?

[Daley shakes his head.]

The stone? Tallest stone as far as the eye can see?

[Daley waves him away.]

It's too high?

DALEY

[shakes his head] Now I'm not talking about him being a white man. I'm the only one knows that. They're gonna ask why that word.

CYRUS

[lifts his eyes and begins to recite.] "In memory of Anna Sanders . . ."

[Daley looks at his own sheet of paper as Cyrus recites.]

"Mother of Cyrus Webster and consort . . ."

DALEY

That's it . . . that's the one.

CYRUS

C-o-n-s-o-r-t

[Eliza enters and stands beside Cyrus.]

c-o-n- [To Daley] Harvard man . . .

DALEY

[waves his hand and begins to write] I can hear them now: "C-o-n-s-o-r-t. That something Christian, or what?"

CYRUS

[steps in front of Eliza] I'm afraid I don't quite understand, Major.

DALEY

You know what I mean. "Were they or weren't they?" That's how they'll put it ...

CYRUS

Good afternoon, Major Daley.

DALEY

You know how they are around here, the Rebs, how they talk and carry on... Hope it's worth all the trouble.

[Cyrus walks Daley to the door.]

CYRUS

Good afternoon, Major.

SCENE TWO

ELIZA

Thought you were from around here.

PATTI

I was born here.

ELIZA

Can't say as I've heard your name.

PATTI

[examines things in room] If you hear my name, please let me know. I was born out here. At Birney Spring. but nobody knows my name. My mother and three of us were sold away. My father stayed behind, did iron work for pay. Saved every penny to buy us back. When he had the money, he went back to look for us. We were gone. Sold away again. There's something in me, burning, this need, old desire, keeps coming back. I'd give anything to see my mother again. (beat) Whose things are these?

ELIZA

I beg your pardon.

PATTI

All these things. [goes from thing to thing. picks up a picture, then a mirror.]

ELIZA

Our family things.

PATTI

And this!

ELIZA

Family. **(takes mirror from her.)**

PATTI

I want to hear your stories. I'm here now and I want to
know it all.

ELIZA

 Simpse's Pa's been arranging things. Family things. He's
got a story or two to tell. If you allow quite a bit of time.

PATTI

Mister Cyrus?

ELIZA

Look at this. He pulled out everything he could find.
They're not usually out this way. He's been taking
inventory.

PATTI

They're lovely things. **[goes to Cyrus's desk]**

ELIZA

Topsy turvy. **[goes to a picture]** Things all out of place.
Not the way they usually are. **[turns it around]** Upside
down.

PATTI

 They aren't usually this way?

ELIZA

Simpses's pa has his personal business. He's laying out his
things. You'll see. We have our things around here. Just
like everybody else. **(beat)** You ask an awful lot of
questions, don't you?

PATTI

Ma'am?

ELIZA

Where'd you meet my Simpse?

PATTI

I was singing at Roger Williams.

ELIZA

But how'd you meet him?

PATTI

There was a tea for the students. Simpse… **[laughs]** He
knew my songs by heart. He was the last one to leave.

ELIZA

That Simpse, once he gets a notion.

PATTI

We're both that way.

ELIZA

You don't say? A young woman traveling alone. You go
around by yourself from town to town.

PATTI

I've always traveled. I tried to sing up North. The doors
were closed.

ELIZA

So you're planning to stay in a little town like this. Not go
from place to place? What about your singing?

PATTI

I'll sing right here. I can still go to Nashville. They'll have me there. I'll sing around the South. Simpse won't mind.

ELIZA

When you're tired of our little town, will you leave Simpse and go off again? Find yourself another beau?

PATTI

I'll never leave.

SCENE THREE

**[Sitting room of Webster home later the same
day. Cyrus comes out with a tray. He and Eliza
sit at the table drinking coffee.]**

CYRUS

Soon as I take care of these lots, put my own house in
order.

ELIZA

Cyrus . . .

CYRUS

Questioning my own mother's last wishes!

ELIZA

But Cyrus, she never talked that way.

CYRUS

I'll see to her memory in a manner befitting the high esteem
in which she was held. "Son, don't ever forget me--
remember me always." I'll make a place for all the
Websters.

ELIZA

Cyrus . . .

CYRUS

Dolly, Dolly . . . [Cyrus goes over and holds her to him.]
we'll be alright— **[Cyrus is arranging papers on his desk
as Eliza looks on.]** A free man can write his own will.
After I take care of these lots, I'll get my will written, put
my own house in order.

ELIZA
[Eliza is bending over Cyrus as he sits at his desk.]
Those words..on your mother's grave? **[points to paper]**

CYRUS

Eliza, Eliza . . .

ELIZA

How do you know she'd want that?

CYRUS

She'd want it.

ELIZA

But Cyrus, it's just not Christian. I mean . . . things happen
and all. Long as I can remember, we have had our hard
times . . . but putting all that on her tombstone . . .

CYRUS

Cyrus Webster's free to say what he wants to say. If they
knew what I knew. **[chuckles]** My own pa, Israel Grant. A
white man. Bold, woden't he?

ELIZA

Cyrus, folks don't usually come right out with it.

CYRUS

They did.

ELIZA

But Cyrus, how do you know?

CYRUS

This man knows. **[pounds his chest]** Can't forget him.
Israel Grant, my own Pa. Saw my mother in a wagon
'round bout 1812 right on the Ohio-Kentucky border.

A cold January day...she was working for his brother
Frank. They come to talking, just like this. **[stares at Eliza
intently.]**

**[Israel descends the stairs and pauses half-way
down; his expression is dejected.]**

She'd run outside to tend the crops; Ol' Israel Grant, he'd
run right after her. Didn't know no better, neither one of
em. Pretty soon, they're meetin' in secret . . . couldn't
marry but they run off together and lived the best they
could. I'll put it on her tomb. I'll stand up to every last . . .
Dolly--**[kisses her hand]**

ELIZA
Folks, they're usually more practical.

CYRUS
I saw them together...I could tell that's what she wanted.
[shakes sheet of paper]
Soon as I get our family plot together, I'll see to my own
papers. Right here...I'll list it all--every room. Let's see--that
bureau over there, that, and that looking glass, **[writing]**
one picture with Noah's ark. And the straw hat? You know
the one.

ELIZA
Cyrus, you gave that away last Fourth of July.

CYRUS
That's right. That's right. I recall a brass kettle, not the one
in the kitchen, not that one, one small with an arm that goes
like so.

ELIZA

It's up in the attic.

CYRUS

Exactly. One wardrobe, the teakettle, one large jar and the
rest of the smoothing irons. What about my sausage
grinder? I cranked that handle many a day...good use,
mighty good use.

ELIZA

That old thing? You know you gave it to Major Daley,
swapped it for the chess set.

CYRUS

Ol' Daley's loss there. His loss alright.

ELIZA

But, Cyrus, what about the acreage? All the crop? You
think Simpse is ready to settle down?

CYRUS

Let's see. I'll divide up the tobacco...How would it go?

ELIZA

That girl Patti. No telling how long she'll stay. And
Israel...acting all contrary.

CYRUS

One trunk packed with tobacco, as full as it will hold on a
damp day.

ELIZA

Cyrus! If you start dividing up things . . .

CYRUS

And I don't want any fussing. **[begins to make notes]**

ELIZA

Cyrus Webster--when you get a grand notion in your head, you won't rest till you see it through. Five lots and two sons. Divide it up and make it all come out equal? Besides, a will? Who knows what could happen? A piece of paper, suppose it falls into the wrong hands?

CYRUS

Supposin'! Supposin' it does? A fella can't make his plans on what might happen. Liza, it's the principle of the thing.

ELIZA

You think they'll let a colored man put his name in the record book? Sign his name down to the courthouse?

CYRUS

The folks at the courthouse try to get me to sign an "x," I'll set 'em straight. Cyrus Webster's own pa taught him to read and write, hid 'im in the cellar and taught him his lesson.

ELIZA

Lord ha'mercy.

[Israel enters and stands on the side.]

CYRUS

We'll just have to put our heads together. **[moves closer]. Cyrus kisses Eliza, then kisses her hand.]** Take my land away? Never. You hear me, Eliza? I said never. Cyrus Webster's free to do what he wants to do, **[holds Eliza]** say whatever he wants to say. Feel the spirit...

ELIZA

And he doesn't need to say a thing about consorting.

[Cyrus holds Eliza. Looks at her intently.]

ISRAEL

Didn't 'spect to see my own folks courtin' so early in the day. I declare I think Pa's smitten.

[Cyrus turns to see Israel.]

CYRUS

Israel Grant Webster. Boy, you spyin' on your own folks. Well, it's legal. It's all legal.

ISRAEL

Pa's got the junebug sure enough.

ELIZA

Your Pa's composing his will.

ISRAEL

Didn't mean to come in on you, Pa. The way you were carryin' on, thought I was walkin' in on the Bard. Now I know where Simpse gets his grand style.

ELIZA

Israel...teasing, your Pa's all excited about your brother Simpse, dreaming about marrying Miss Patti... all her singing on the Fourth . . . Cyrus, you s'pose she 'lows a piano with the Lord's music?

CYRUS

A piano? We'll be steppin' high this Fourth and Patti'll be marchin' right along with the rest of the folks.

ISRAEL

The rest of the folks? Pa, depending on the company, you might not be able to hear her at all.

ELIZA
Singing the Lord's music on the Fourth of July. How can the Lord hear you with all that going on?

[We can hear Patti practicing.]

CYRUS
Last Fourth of July, the Black Swan sang. Sang in Nashville, right in the front of the congregation.

[Cyrus laughs and pats his knee. Eliza scowls.]

ISRAEL
What's singing got to do with working a tobacco farm? You think Simpse is really gon' marry that girl? She's here now. Come sun up, she could run off, leave Simpse empty-handed.

[Israel is growing impatient; one can see that he is at loose ends. Simpse enters carrying a bag.]

ISRAEL
Glory be, Simpse gettin' married.

[Israel brightens up for a moment and grasps Simpse's shoulder affectionately. Henry Garrett follows him, bringing in bags, setting them down and returning with more bags. When the men open the door, we can hear noises, a clash of voices from outside, the sounds of a working group.]

ISRAEL
Is that all the bags we packed?

CYRUS

Henry Garrett--

[Garrett leaves again and returns.]

ELIZA

Garrett.

ISRAEL

Henry Garrett, you and your boy bring in all our bags?

[Garrett nods and leaves.]

CYRUS

Garrett's got plenty of sense, plenty of sense.

ISRAEL

I know he has. Pa, how many bags Garrett's s'posed to
leave for us?

CYRUS

Never you mind about that.

ISRAEL

You trust a sharecropper to count out his bags and leave the
rest alone? Pa?

CYRUS

Garrett's got his share. He takes his. Same as before. The
rest is ours.

ISRAEL

You didn't write it down?

CYRUS

Don't have to. Don't have to write everything down.

ISRAEL

Then I'll do what I have to do. That's right, Pa. From now
on, I'll divvy up Garrett's tobacco myself.

**[Cyrus stares at Israel in disbelief. Simpse
enters.]**

SIMPSE

Pa, Old man Daley rode past me, took one look, and shook
his head. Now when a Union man starts shakin' his head
. . . Pa, what you say to old man Daley? Pa?

[Cyrus turns away.]

Guess I better watch out. He might be plannin' my stone
too.

ELIZA

Simpse, your Pa's thinkin' hard. Making arrangements for
your grandmother's . . . monument.

**[Simpse goes over and starts poking through the
papers.]**

Never you mind about that. **[walks him to the door]** Go
find your brother. We need to get the tobacco together for
market day. **[calls out the door]** Israel?

CYRUS

[calls out] Israel! What's that boy doing now? The four of
us, we'll go on out to Birney Springs, first thing in the
morning, finish bagging up our crop. We've got bags full
of tobacco, Eliza. Look down in the cellar. Bags as full as
they'll hold on a damp day.

[Patti is practicing in the background.]

SCENE FOUR

[Later in the day, an outdoor scene. Israel
appears, dances around awkwardly, as if at loose
ends. He is uncomfortable, a little edgy, but trying
to give the appearance of being at ease. Tom
Garrett enters. Israel spots him immediately and
calls him over. We can hear other voices in the
background.]

ISRAEL

Thomas Carl Garrett.

TOM GARRETT

Whoaaa, Israel. [shades his eyes with his hands]

ISRAEL

Where you headin' off to?

TOM GARRETT

Wait a minute, from way down the road. The way you was
lookin, kinda struttin'-like. You know from the back.
Couldn't see nothing but that ol' jacket o yourn. Boy . . . I
thought you was a white boy. Say who that white boy
comin down the road?

ISRAEL

[pulls away angrily] You know better'n that.

TOM GARRETT

I know I know better but just the way you was walkin. Like
you own the road. I coulda sworn...

ISRAEL

Tom Garrett, you 'bout to start somethin.

**[Tom Garrett laughs and the two of them grab
each other and wrestle around. Israel crouches
and punches at Garrett. They pretend to be
soldiers.]**

Hey Garrett, remember Peach Orchard Hill? The Battle of
Nashville? You gone get whipped all over again.

**[The two of them break apart. Garrett is angry
now.]**

TOM GARRETT

Yep, I think he does think he's a white boy. Yessir. He's
gone plumb crazy. **(beat)** We beat you good.

ISRAEL

You ain't beat nobody, Garrett. Here's fifteen cents. Go on
into town. Buy yourself some firecrackers. Fourth a July
comin'! Put what's left in your pocket.

TOM GARRETT

I don't need your money.

**[Garrett throws money at Israel. Runs off. Israel
laughs loudly.]**

**[We can hear voices approaching. One of the
voices, a man's, is loud and celebratory. Israel
hides in a clump of bushes and watches quietly as
Henry Garrett and his son Tom work. Both bend
down to examine a pile of tobacco. Israel watches
them from the bushes as the Garretts move on.
Simpse and Cyrus enter. The three, Simpse,
Cyrus, and Israel begin to tend the crop. Israel's
rifle is off to the side. Simpse is raking the
ground. Simpse and Israel are working together.]**

ISRAEL

[To Simpse] So I come marchin' down the stairs and
there's Pa kissing Ma's hand like so, "Dolly...," breathin'
hard like some young rascal fresh from Nashville...

SIMPSE

The Webster charm.

ISRAEL

Going on about Grandma's monument. **[hitting a rock
with his rake, pounding as Simpse talks]** And how he
was going to write a will. Piece of paper. You think a
colored man's will means anything?

SIMPSE

Did you see the way Patti lifts her skirt when she walks?

ISRAEL

Boy, did you hear me? Pa wants to write a will. They'll
laugh him out of the courthouse.

SIMPSE

Then she lifts it a little higher, like she's going to fall or
something, catches herself like so, and she's up and
standing tall.

ISRAEL

Patti, Patti, that's all you know. You hear what I said? You
think they'll let a black man's hands soil the courthouse
books?

SIMPSE

Don't you let Pa hear you talk that way!

ISRAEL

Wake up, Simpse. I'm talking about the real world. Look at me, boy. This world, not the one out there somewhere, the one right here.

SIMPSE

Israel, this is me, Simpse, I'm back from the war, grown, mindin' my own affairs.

ISRAEL

Getting smart, huh? Ol' Simpse Webster, flyin' high, gonna jump the broom.

[Spotlight on Patti sweeping the floor.]

SIMPSE

Did I ever tell you how it was, Israel? How it was with the two of us? You know what I mean.

[Israel pulls away.]

Me and Patti, seems like I've been knowing her all my life. The way it was with you and Caroline. You understand, don't you?

ISRAEL

Her? She's gone.

SIMPSE

But you understand, don't you?

ISRAEL

I think I do, Simpse. Now let's see if I remember this right. Our Tennessee belle has you up on a cloud. She's got you all addled, can't put one foot in front of the other without trippin' over yourself. Don't you know what she'll do to you? She'll turn you to mush, then cut and run.

SIMPSE

She sings just like a bird.

ISRAEL

A bird? What kind of bird?

SIMPSE

The loveliest bird in the sky.

ISRAEL

That crow over there, she can sing.

SIMPSE

[looks at bird wistfully] I imagine she can.

ISRAEL

He imagines she can. [dances with a rake] Oh, Simpse darling, hold me close.

SIMPSE

The way that girl's drawn up so tight, sometimes it's a wonder she doesn't faint. [Simpse shoves the rake at Israel.]

ISRAEL

She's puny alright. [dances with rake] Too puny if you ask me.

SIMPSE

Wait till Patti sings on the Fourth. You'll hear the power. [Simpse starts to sing] Up at Roger Williams, Patti and her classmates didn't want to go around singing jubilees.

ISRAEL
And what does our bride want to sing?

SIMPSE
Verdi.
[Simpse imitates a parade march]

ISRAEL
Verdi . . . an Eyetalian to boot. Have mercy.

SIMPSE
You heard me.

ISRAEL
Verdi? Who wants to hear you all singing that?

SIMPSE
When they arrived at the auditorium, not a black face there,
the president of the college said, "Here, you can sing
anything on this list"——every jubilee you ever heard. It's a
good thing Simpse Webster wasn't there. All she wanted to
do was sing her solo.

ISRAEL
Verdi! Lord have mercy.

**[Cyrus is checking his bags of tobacco off to the
side.]**

CYRUS
Boy, don't you take the Lord's name in vain. Where's Tom
Garrett?

ISRAEL
Sent him into town. Git some firecrackers. Fourth of July
right around the corner . . Come on, Pa, who's going to pay

good money to hear black folks sing Verdi? You think
they want to hear her singing like that? Don't care how
pretty a singer she is.

SIMPSE

She's a pretty one alright. Did you see the way Patti wears
her hat to one side, sets her off, doesn't it? With that big
feather . . . purple.   [winds his fingers around his head]

ISRAEL

Patti could sing from now to next year, all over town. Sing
in every field.

[Hands Simpse the rake forcefully. Simpse
accepts it immediately. On the other side of the
field, a spotlight falls on Patti. We see what
Simpse imagines. Patti sings an aria or art song
from the time period. Up and under. Patti sings
off and on.]

SIMPSE

[to Israel] I'll tell you this. Nobody's going to tell Simpse
Webster how to sing, nobody around here leastways.

CYRUS

[Cyrus enters, goes over and hands Simpse a bag] That's
right. Who's gonna tell Simpse what to do?

SIMPSE

Wait till you see us, we'll be dressed to go to town, all our
finery.

ISRAEL

Finery? Look at that bunch of crows flying over the trees.
All slicked up.

[Simpse looks]

Look at em, big, ornery, black, dancing, jazzing, loud as they want to be.

[Crows make a honking sound.]

SIMPSE
[Puts hands to lips.] Sing soft now.

ISRAEL
[To Cyrus] You know this one's blind. **[Points to Simpse.]** He's in love. Can't see a thing.

SIMPSE
Sing on, brother crow.

[Crows sing louder.]

All my pretty chickens . . .

ISRAEL
Pretty?

[Crows sing louder.]

Watch out now, you're talking to Israel Webster--a free man. You hear me, brother crow? I've always been free, damn you. I was born free--just didn't know it. **[laughs and dances around in a circle.]**

CYRUS
[hands Israel a rake.] He was born free. Just had to be reminded.

ISRAEL

You ever here tell about crows? They're smart, damn smart. You know a crow can find his man, faster than a Yank crossing the enemy line.

SIMPSE

"How now, you secret, black and midnight hags! What is't you do?"

ISRAEL

The war's over. We won it, we won the whole damn thing.

SIMPSE

They'll say you seen the Webster boys . . . The Webster boys? Oh they're off dining on pheasant, bouillon and ham.

CYRUS

[sorting bags] They'll say you seen Simpse Webster?

SIMPSE

Simpse Webster? Oh he's off performin' at the Shakespeare Society.

ISRAEL

Finery and all.

CYRUS

Fallin' off the balcony of Mt. Lebanon Church.

[The brothers laugh.]

On the Fourth of July.

SIMPSE

Some day I'm gonna have more money than any man in Maury County.

ISRAEL

Better watch out, ol' crow, they'll say you're trying to start the war all over again.

SIMPSE

[points to himself, steps forward] Private Simpson T. Webster; **[points to Israel]** Captain Israel B. Webster . **[Israel picks up his rifle and stands at attention. Cyrus is silent.]** Come on Pa . . . General Cyrus John Webster.

[Israel and Simpse dodge around and box at each other. While they are playing around, Tom Garrett enters carrying a rifle on a strap. Patti stops singing.]

TOM GARRETT

Well, well, caught him with his clan.

ISRAEL

The Klan? That's your folks, Garrett. Ain't none of mine.

[Tom Garrett walks around, stops in front of Cyrus, pauses then goes to Simpse, pauses, then stops in front of Israel, but does not speak to him.]

TOM GARRETT

Howdy, Simpse. Right nice day, ain't it? Uncle Cyrus, when you gonna bring me those schoolbooks, ones over to Mount Lebanon. You ain't hidin' 'em, are ye? **[To Israel]** Howdy do, Israel. Those bales a tobacco too heavy for ye? I can take it off your hands.

[Simpse and Cyrus laugh with Tom Garrett. When Israel turns and glares, they stop right away.]

ISRAEL

Pa, you never told me I had a long-lost cousin. Mighty
tender, ain't it. Which side of the family? Let's see, North or
South?

TOM GARRETT

Right nice jacket you wearin'. **[to Cyrus]** Lot better lookin'
than some I seen. **[glances at Israel's Union jacket,
laughs]** Israel...soldier's coat. You know those soldiers.

SIMPSE

[nudges Israel] Peach Orchard Hill.

[Cyrus holds Israel back.]

TOM GARRETT

Sure is some pretty singing over to your house, Uncle
Cyrus. Hear you-all plannin' a big to-do, the Fourth.

ISRAEL

That's right, a big to-do. Sing a little song.   **[Israel hums
"Yellow Rose of Texas."]** You ought to come, Garrett.

CYRUS

Whole town's welcome.

ISRAEL

Yes, indeed. I'm issuin' you a special invitation.

TOM GARRETT

You know some days--I get up, look all around, feel like
there's somethin' I oughta have, somethin' oughta be mine.
[Picks up a pile of tobacco.] You know what it's like?
Like I can see all the way to Birney Spring--That. That over
there, that ought be mine, all the way down to....I swear the
whole world's gone crazy. Where you get this bag of

tobacco? I swear I left that bag over there.

ISRAEL

That bag over there?

TOM GARRETT

Seems a man can hardly keep up with what he's got without some durn fool comin along and grabbin' what's his. Wake up some days, look in the windowpane, wonder if it's me. **[feels face]**

ISRAEL

Come 'ere. Let me look at you. Close up.

[Tom Garrett eyes him skeptically.]

Yeh, that's right. Same hair, same crooked part on the side, scar you got fallin out of that apple tree. You're Tom Garrett alright, your pa, Henry Garrett, worked our land from the time he sucked a sugar tit. Same Garretts rented our land before the war...I 'spects I know you.

TOM GARRETT

That bag of tobacco--that's mine.

CYRUS

Smart man, your pa, used to say, my boy Tom, when he was a baby, see two apples, had two hands, figured he needed them both.

TOM GARRETT

You just might be right, Mr. Cyrus Webster. You just might be right.

ISRAEL

Give the man his bag of tobacco. **[passes bag to Simpse.]**

TOM GARRETT

That one over there.

ISRAEL

That one. **[passes bag to Simpse]**

TOM GARRETT

Yesterday, sun hardly up, left a pile over there.

ISRAEL

Pa, you see a stray bag of tobacco round here?

CYRUS

No stray bags a tobacco. I see a few strays, but no stray bags.

TOM GARRETT

That's my bag.

ISRAEL

One going to market in the morning? Pa, you sending that to market?

CYRUS

All that tobacco over there. It's ready for market.

ISRAEL

See all that tobacco. It's going out first thing in the morning.

TOM GARRETT

Morning? They don't let you go up in the morning.

ISRAEL

Don't? Says who?

TOM GARRETT
[ignores him, to Cyrus, pointing to Israel.] Don't he
know he's got to wait till we're finished?

CYRUS
He knows no such thing...no such thing. All the Websters .
. . early birds.

DALEY
[enters with Cyrus's paper work] Cyrus, I brought your
paperwork back.

[Cyrus looks around nervously.]
ISRAEL
Pa's afraid to leave us alone, Major Daley. Says when he's
gone, the trouble starts.

DALEY
Me and your Pa got business to do. Look at all this. You
boys've got plenty to do.

[Cyrus and Daley confer.]

SIMPSE
You heard him, Garrett. Get busy.

TOM GARRETT
You all? You think you gon' always have all this? Close
your eyes. Now open 'em again . . . it's all gone.

ISRAEL
[walks around him] Now will you look at this? Yep, I
'spects I know you. Man rents land from me.

TOM GARRETT
Rent it from your Pa.

ISRAEL

Oh, 'scuse me. Man's pa rents land from my pa. Works on
my land.

CYRUS

Our land.

ISRAEL

Works our land. Tells me what he's going to do with our
tobacco.

**[Simpse goes over and examines bag of tobacco,
smiling.]**

ISRAEL

Somebody . . . find this soldier's bag of tobaccy.

[Simpse and Israel look around.]

SIMPSE

Captain Webster. Call the infantry. Tom Garrett, front and
center. Where are we? That's right. Peach Orchard Hill!

**[Salutes Simpse; Tom Garrett freezes. Israel's
rifle at his side.]**

SIMPSE

Iiiiiima cocococolored color bearer. **[grabs Israel by the
shoulder]** Yes, I am. Remember Ol' Ed. Ed Daniel
Calloway. Always did stutter, said I'm a colored color
bearer. Folks say What you doin' over there, Ed? Ed say,
you know he stuttered like so...iiiima colored color bearer
and he'd carried that banner--whoooo

[Cyrus strides towards Simpse.]

CYRUS
Look around you. Don't you boys know the war's over?

SIMPSE
Pa, you can't imagine it . . . never saw so many men die so
fast...Crockett and Mike, Otis and Ed—[**calls out**] Ed. He
didn't make a sound . All of a sudden along came Israel
Webster, [Embraces Israel; the two start wrestling around]
picked up Ed's banner—

**[Israel grabs a bag of tobacco. Garrett walks
towards him.]**

Your boy Israel, Pa, he carried that big flag, Eighteenth
Regiment U.S. Colored Infantry. Those ladies from
Murfreesboro sure did sew up a pretty banner and Israel
carried it all the way up Peach Orchard Hill. They say when
you walked back down your foot never touched the ground
. . . all the colored boys.

[Simpse and Israel start to sing softly.]
Glory, glory hallelujah.

**[Simpse and Israel clasp hands and hug each
other, then start to wrestle around, boyish,
vigorous, not aware of their own strength. Israel
holds up bag of tobacco. Tries to pass it to
Simpse.]**

GARRETT
[**pushes Simpse out of the way**] You think all this is
yours?

**[Israel lunges at Garrett. Garrett falls to the
ground. Cyrus pulls him back up.]**

You think you gon' keep all this? Close your eyes. Now open 'em again. It's all gone.

> **[Israel holds his gun at his side. Simpse stands behind him. Garrett grabs his gun and aims it at Israel]**

DALEY

You heard him. Look all around you. Don't you boys know the war's over

> **[Tom Garrett lowers gun, then leaves.]**

SCENE FIVE

[The next day at Birney Springs. Henry Garret carries in a podium. Cyrus is getting ready for the Fourth of July celebration. Israel enters from the side. He makes a tapping noise on the shed, stops and makes the same noise again.]

CYRUS

When in the course of human events . . . **[doesn't hear tapping]** . . . it becomes necessary . . . **[hears a noise and jumps around, reaches for his rifle. Cyrus and Israel are face to face.]**

ISRAEL

So that's what farmers do when they get through cleaning the hogpens--practice the Fourth of July oration.

CYRUS

When they get through.

[Israel goes over and picks up a bucket.]

Just tend to your own business, that's all.

ISRAEL

This is my business, Pa. Simpse and Patti, settling down, so they tell me... **[reaches for Cyrus's rifle. Cyrus picks it up and sets it aside.]**

CYRUS

You're the one had better settle down--you and Tom Garrett. You got us all worried.

ISRAEL

Me? You're the one they ought to worry about.

CYRUS

The kind of trouble you're in. Israel...

ISRAEL

You think the ones like Tom Garrett'll ever listen to you? I know, I know, if they didn't stay on our land, they'd starve. Look at the way Tom Garrett walks around here. You'd think he owned the place.

[For a moment, they come together.]

Pa, I've seen that rifle before, the same one you keep in the back of the church. When you go over to teach, you bring it with you.

CYRUS

Ol' Pol Parrot, gettin in folk's business.

ISRAEL

Pa's got the biggest rifle, but I'm the one everybody's complaining about. Oughta live up North. Give youall some peace.

CYRUS

You're not going anywhere.

ISRAEL

I'm not?

CYRUS

I won't let you.

ISRAEL

You won't let me. That's right. "Easy, Israel, easy, don't go getting mad. Tom Garrett and his boys play you for the fool. Take it a little bit longer. Wait till Judgment Day . . .

you'll get your reward."

CYRUS
You don't have to wait that long. Look around you, that stretch of land over there, bright leaf, far as the eye can see. That's yours.

[Israel turns away.]

You think I built all this up, so you could go runnin' off?

ISRAEL
[Israel turns back to Cyrus] But Pa, **[they embrace]** I'm not like you and Ma.

CYRUS
Don't need to be.

ISRAEL
I just can't do it.

CYRUS
Watch yourself. That's all you need to do.

ISRAEL
I've seen you. You do your farming, once a week you teach school, at church, so they can't tell what you're doing. Teaching in broad daylight! When you walk back to your desk, you hide your rifle. You stand by the window, book in one hand, rifle in the other. Cyrus Webster, hero, and never been to war. Never had to sit in a ditch all night, waiting to see if the Lord would spare him--this time.

CYRUS
[bows] I thank you, Captain Webster.

ISRAEL

Captain--what did that ever get me?

CYRUS

How many colored soldiers fought in the war?   You were a captain.

ISRAEL

A captain. You knew the company commander,

CYRUS

A colored captain.

ISRAEL

Had ol' man Daley's brother talk to Mr. Arnell, he put in a good word. I never did any of it on my own. Never. You hear me. I've never done a thing on my own.

CYRUS

Stop your whining. You think you're the first one had something fixed up that way? Daley's nephew, Harvard boy, wasn't he? You, Israel G. Webster, one colored boy, the only one I ever heard of, made it that far.

ISRAEL

Shoes polished . . . button that collar..and look at me now. Getting screamed at by a poor dumb white boy, had his first bath outside an army tent, but he can talk bad to a darkie.

CYRUS

As the educated class--

ISRAEL

Pa, Pa . . .

CYRUS

It's up to us to establish an atmosphere of tolerance--
reason.

ISRAEL

Listen to the orator.

CYRUS

Don't you backtalk me.

ISRAEL

Might offend your delicate sensibilities.

CYRUS

A colored man with sensibilities. That's me. Too much
book learning, too high faluting for my own good,

[Israel shakes his head.]

nothing but a fool underneath--isn't that what they say?

ISRAEL

[rushes to Cyrus] Better never say it to me.

CYRUS

One thing I know, I know trouble when I see it, the kind
you're in, Israel Grant Webster. I can't have you leaving.
Your pa's expecting great things out of you.

ISRAEL

You called me captain, Pa. Alright then, I want my respect.
Walk to the head of the line. Maybe the war did spoil me,
but I can't go back now. **[beat]** I know, Pa. I know. But
you weren't really in the army.

CYRUS

Oh yes, I was too old to go to war. For a black man, Israel, there's not much difference between war and peace. When my word's as good as a white man's. When I can write a will just like a white man, then there'll be peace. Everything you see around you. Our lan'. At least, that's what it says in the record book. My pa, Ol' Israel Grant, he told me "here, son, here's all the money I saved for you, every penny you earned doing chores about the home. You earned it. It's yours! Listen close. Go on over to Tennessee, look for a man named Daley, he'll take you down to the courthouse, see you buy some good plots of land. You won't have to worry about a thing!" Ha! That's what my pa told me. The day I bought my first plot of land, ol' man war stopped right at my door. Invited himself in. When the big war finally came, I was tired of it. No man's fought harder than I have. I'll die easy, son, if I know this land's here for you and your brother.

ISRAEL

For me? There's nothing here for me. **[holds up empty pail]**

CYRUS

That gal Caroline…forget about her. Son, you'll find somebody else.

ISRAEL

Caroline!?? Pa**…[shakes head].** Pa…She's…

CYRUS

…Son, she's gone. You can make a good life here.

ISRAEL

Pa, you wanna know what's on my mind? Listen close. After what I've been through-- Peach Orchard Hill, The Battle of Nashville--you think I'm gonna let some redneck call me names?

CYRUS

Peach Orchard Hill, Peach Orchard Hill. That's all you and
Simpse talk about . . . climbing the hill and marching down
with dead boy's bodies under your feet, especially when
you've got Tom Garrett for an audience. When the two of
you were boys, you and Garrett fought all the time--"That's
my cup of water, that's my stick." When I saw the two of
you out there yesterday, it was like you'd never changed.

ISRAEL

I went there expecting to come back a hero.

CYRUS

That's right. . . You were happy before the war. You fought
like hell and now you're mad. What were you trying to do
yesterday?

ISRAEL

Pa, look over there, look at that rifle you carry.

CYRUS

But I don't go around town letting everybody know about
it. Boasting, acting all loud. You think you can destroy
Garrett? Well, do you? Israel, tell me, tell me what the
white folks call our hill? Go on, say it--Mink Slide.

[Israel laughs out loud.]

They say we're like minks--all that precious oil God gave
us, we can slide, quick as lightning, straight to the bottom
of the hill, crawl around . . . all night . . .

ISRAEL

Pa, you ought to stick to your books.

CYRUS

You know about it.

ISRAEL

About what?

CYRUS

About lovin'. Mink Slide, drink, cut each other up a little, and love. Is that what you want? Isn't it enough to feed and clothe your family, go to church on Sunday?

ISRAEL

And fall in love. "Go on home, boy. The war's over. Hold your lady in your arms. Wait a minute. Your sweetheart's gone."

CYRUS

Can't stop looking back, can you?

ISRAEL

You're right. I can't, can I? Sing the motto: "Roger Williams forever more." Pa knew the company commander, so I went to war. **[beat]** Remember how it was before the war? How I went off, the happiest man alive? Ma fixed me a sack of beaten biscuits. You gave me the little Shakespeare. All your favorite speeches circled.

[Cyrus laughs.]

I made a promise that night. Me and Simpse, we were gonna come back heroes . . . heroes.

CYRUS

But you are, Israel, you are.

[Lights fade.]

SCENE SIX

Setting: a room with a featherbed piled high with mattresses. Nightclothes are neatly arranged at the foot of the bed. Bed clothing, walls in primal, basic colors, wheats, straws, off-whites with complementary earthtones. Bed clothes, quilts and a brown plaid Indian blanket are folded neatly at the foot of the featherbed. Cyrus and Eliza are alone in the room. The crickets can be heard chirping outside. Cyrus is sitting on the bed wearing a full set of long underwear. Eliza removes her outer clothing only to reveal a full set of sleeveless underclothes. She sits on the floor and hands Cyrus a hairbrush. He begins to brush her hair.

ELIZA

He won't take that coat off, will he?

CYRUS

[turns Eliza's head] This way, Dolly.

ELIZA

Israel, he won't take off that coat.

CYRUS

Leetle bit over. Now. [adusts Eliza's head]

ELIZA

The way that boy looks you'd think the war was still going on. Babies together. Israel and Tom Garrett. Who woulda thought they'd fight like this?

CYRUS

Call on Liza Webster, she'll tame the savage beast.

ELIZA

Born in the same year, seven days apart. Israel first, then
Garrett. Guess I shoulda known. His own ma--sick off and
on--real frail. That boy, Tom Garrett sucked with a fury,
cried night and day. Never could get enough. **(beat)** Why
do you suppose Israel wears that jacket every day?

CYRUS

Boy's proud of his soldiering.

ELIZA

If I had my way, there'd be no celebration this year.

CYRUS

No celebration? Why, we'll light up the sky.

ELIZA

It would be just like Israel to start something up at the
picnic. Did you ever notice those looks Israel gives Patti
out of the corner of his eye? I wish he wouldn't follow after
her so. Makes me tired.

CYRUS

The boy's out of sorts. His own girl runnin' off, marrying
while he was away at war. Dolly, you got enough on you
already . . .

ELIZA

I wish he'd stop followin' after that Patti.

CYRUS

Simpse'll be marryin' her before you know it.

ELIZA

And his brother'll be fighting all over town.

CYRUS

You just wait till the Fourth, you'll see. I can hear the folks
now--"Landsakes, yonder goes Israel Webster in all his
finery!" He'll dress to beat the band. And hold on, there
goes Simpson and his bride-to-be . . . that girl's the spittin'
image of my own Ma. Pure-blooded African.

ELIZA

Cyrus, about this consort . . .

CYRUS

A king's lady, that's what.

ELIZA

But you s'pose folks'll hold it against 'em?

CYRUS

Anna Sanders and Israel Grant? Who'd bless that union?
Not a courthouse in the land. Coulda walked on foot, 200
miles in any direction . . . a white man married to a colored
woman. I'll put that on her tombstone--consort to Israel
Grant.

ELIZA

But Cyrus, that's a king's lady.

CYRUS

That's right. He was the king and she was queen. **[holds
Eliza]** I'll tell you that. A queen, that's how he treated her.
[hugs Eliza. Eliza laughs.]

ELIZA

But she never wrote anything down.

CYRUS

That's what I been saying. That's what I been saying. She
didn't write anything down. That's why her own son's got
to set the record straight. A cold January day, she was
working for his brother Frank. They come to talking just,
just like this...

ELIZA

Cyrus, I know this story by heart. **[beat]** That Patti ought to
go off with her own folks.

CYRUS

Mother, I'm surprised at you.

ELIZA

Well she oughta, besides Simpse's too young. He's just
getting his strength back. Why can't she sing "Swing
Low"? The part that goes . . .
> **[Eliza hums "Swing Low"] [Cyrus and Eliza
> sing together. Fade out.]**

> **[Soft lights on Patti and Israel outside. Patti is
> repotting a plant. She tries to pull the roots a
> part. Israel stands beside her.**

ISRAEL

You'll never get them out that way.

PATTI

Don't be too sure of that...

ISRAEL

Those roots go way down there...

PATTI

There. I've got it.

ISRAEL

You think you have.

PATTI

[Patti holds up sections of the plant] Ol' Israel knows everything, doesn't he?

ISRAEL

[Israel grabs Patti's hand] Your scrawny little plant? Anybody can pull that a part. You see that tree over there. You say to yourself couldn't be much to that one little tree. You could put your foot down anywhere around this yard, you're standing on roots, locked tight. Those roots are strong, all spread out, they go deep. Deep. Like me and Simpse...you know... Me and Simpse? I go one way. Simpse, he's right behind me.

[Patti pulls away and keeps digging with her hands]

Turn the other way, there's Simpse, pulling up in the wagon.

[Patti continues.]

No room for anything else to grow. Tight. You better wash off your hands.

PATTI

I know what you think, Israel. I oughta to stick to practicing my songs.

ISRAEL

That's right. Little town like this, it's too dull, not fast enough for the likes of you.

PATTI

I never said anything about leaving.

ISRAEL

You'll leave.

[Patti shakes head.]

Yes, you will. Pack your bags, head up North somewhere.

PATTI

Right here...This is all I need. Sometimes when you're about to give up **...[holds up plant]** There. I've got all of it.

ISRAEL

That's what they all say, "go on--I'll be here." You come back, they're gone.

[Simpse enters unnoticed.]

PATTI

Who gave you the right to tell me about my feelings? You think you can look inside me. See what I'm feeling. Go on. Look. You can't see a thing. Israel, you're all bitter, mad about everything.

[Israel grabs Patti and holds her for a minute.]

ISRAEL

Patti . . .

[Patti pulls away, hesitates, then runs off without noticing Simpse. Simpse approaches Israel.]

SIMPSE

Nashville, the Athens of the South, brings us a gift of incomparable . . .

[walks over to Israel]

Patti's tired. She's been practicing all day, worrying about singing on the Fourth. . . . We need to meet, get all the veterans together. Must be a hundred to two hundred boys ready to march on the Fourth. Right down the square.

ISRAEL

It'll be a hot day for marching.

SIMPSE

Two hundred colored veterans keeping time. Forward ho!

[Israel sits down on a rock.]

Wait till Patti sings for our boys.

[Fadeout. Lights up on Cyrus and Eliza.]

CYRUS

Love is in the air. [scratches Eliza's scalp] Eliza Webster, that woman knows how to work up a plan. At the ready. Yes sir.

ELIZA

You know what they always say, say we don't have any business celebrating the Fourth, say it's not our place, say we . . .

CYRUS

We'll show 'em darkies can celebrate the Fourth just like everybody else. [starts to recite]

ELIZA
You certainly have a way with the Declaration. And your
poems.

CYRUS
After the cakes and pies, when we're all resting, might even
recite a few lines of Gray's "Elegy."

ELIZA
Cyrus--

CYRUS
Yes, Dolly.

ELIZA
Cyrus--

CYRUS
Woman, what you want?

ELIZA
Israel's not going back out to the field. You and Simpse
can bring the rest of the bags in. Cyrus, I don't want Israel
out there fighting with Tom Garrett. Fourth of July's
tomorrow.

CYRUS
All right, Dolly, all right. All right...

FADEOUT

END OF ACT ONE

ACT TWO

SCENE ONE

[A crowd of men, women and children has gathered at Birney Spring for the Fourth of July celebration. The group sings the final stanza of "The Battle Hymn of The Republic," then applauds. Patti and Eliza pass out small flags. We hear cheering in the background. Cyrus goes to the front of the crowd. Tom Garrett is standing off to the side.]

CYRUS

As we celebrate this grand occasion, let us remember that we live in a country of free men. My fellow Tennesseans of good will, when you give thanks for this year's crop, give a special thanks to the colored man. Our labor has built this country, but we'll not be slaves again.

[Clapping, crowd waves flags in the air.]

They'll try to break you. Wear you down, defeat you at every turn, cause you to doubt your ability to feed, clothe, care for your family. When you find that your needs outweigh your ability to provide for the ones you love, turn to the Mutual Benefit Association.

[Unexplained noise in background]

Sometimes a little friend will call you over, whisper in your ear, so and so's doing this, see that one over there, he's got more'n you, how'd he get that? Better come on over and work for me. I'll keep you fed. Ladies and gentlemen, if we quarrel, we'll not quarrel with each other. Stand together. Don't turn against your colored brother. Sister, plant your neighbor's corn. Mend her clothes. Tend her sick. And both your gardens will grow.

[At first Israel and the rest of the family are seated near Cyrus. Before Cyrus can finish his speech, we hear noises in the background. Israel goes over to a clump of bushes and finds Tom Garrett. Spotlight on Israel and Tom Garrett.]

TOM GARRETT

[Laughs a high strange laugh] Hail the conquering hero. **[pretends to salute and aim a rifle. holds a wine bottle in the other hand.]** Ol' Israel's back for more. Woooah, if my boys knew you were out here. Thought your Pa was gonna invite me to the picnic. **[pushes the bottle away]** Come on, have a little watermelon wine---remember when we was boys, how the three of us, me, you, and Simpse used to be? Just like this--   **[Holds three fingers close together]**

ISRAEL

Used to be.

TOM GARRETT

How we used to pretend like we was going up to the hills in Nashville lookin' for sang--good old ginseng? **[Sings ginseng song]** And Simpse would call out "get the pirates over yonder." Had it all laid out . . . me playin' the general and you just an old foot soldier. **[stops for a minute, looks up and smiles]** The three of us'd go fishin' on the Duck River, tell stories 'bout riding all the way round the world, Old Israel's got me dangling alright. Whose side you on, huh? Look, I'll give you two cat-eye marbles for a jar of peaches.

ISRAEL

Don't need no marbles.

TOM GARRETT

Okay. I'll give you one of my squirrel guns for a looking glass. Ma gal, she been after me and after me for one a those.

ISRAEL

I got a squirrel gun.

TOM GARRETT

How about my army knife for your fur hat?

ISRAEL

Got one of those too.

TOM GARRETT

Doggone stingy, ain't he? Come on, I'll trade you for something you ain't got.

[Eliza comes over and shushes the two. They ignore her.]

ISRAEL

Don't need anything . . . specially what you go to give away. When I came back, I brought my horse with me.

[Simpse and Patti come by arm in arm. We hear Eliza's voice calling out.]

ELIZA

Gather for the reading. Boys and girls, the front row--mind your manners.

TOM GARRETT
Come on. [Warmly, as if they were kids again] Let's fight it out.

HENRY GARRETT
[Carrying bottle, yells out, then exits] Both a you. You home now. You hear me. [raises bottle] Boys, the war's over.

ISRAEL
[To Tom Garrett] In case you got a bad memory, you and me we're grown.

TOM GARRETT
You all sure are somethin'--ever since you got back--ain't hardly growed whiskers. Simpse gone and got hisself a bride, you ain't grown at all.

[Israel lunges at Garrett. Spotlight on Cyrus as he recites, stands in front of group.]

CYRUS
"When, in the course of human events, it becomes necessary for one people to dissolve the political bands which have connected them with another..."

[Spotlight on Garrett and Israel arguing.]

ISRAEL
Captain Israel Webster.

TOM GARRETT
They didn't make none of you Captain.

ISRAEL

Did too.

TOM GARRETT

Did not.

[Garrett stops suddenly, laughs, devilishly, as if holding on to some sly secret. Israel lunges forward. Garrett laughs again and jumps out of his way.]

TOM GARRETT

And he's already struttin' just like a peacock--and wouldn't you know it--got a long tail, feathers stickin' straight up. **[Tom reaches for Israel's gun, but Israel jumps back]** Heard about this colored boy just last week. Thought just because he finally got up Peach Orchard Hill at the big fight at Nashville, he could take charge of all a Delphi. Got whipped for sassing.

[Israel lunges at Garrett. Garrett jumps away again.]

Your pa with all that land, one whole side of town, how many children **(holds up both hands)** Nah. Just two. Them Websters making some genuine Durham Smoking Tobacco. Y'all got enough to pass around.

[Spotlight on Cyrus]

CYRUS

"We hold these truths to be self evident, that all men are created equal; that they are endowed by their Creator with certain inalienable rights . . ."

[Back to Garrett and Israel.]

TOM GARRETT

Cap'n Israel thinks he's so smart, got the upper hand. When he goes to jail for sassin' we'll see how smart he is.

ISRAEL

Sassin' ? Lord ha' mercy, boy musta plumb forgot bout the Battle of Nashville. You and Gen'ral Hood, you weren't so big and strong, were you? **[applause, crowd waves flags]** Didn't they tell you? It's the Fourth of July.

CYRUS

"That among these are life, liberty, and the pursuit of happiness."

[Spotlight on Tom Garrett and Israel. Tom Garrett puts his fists up, begins to dance towards Israel. Israel matches him. The shadow boxing continues for a few minutes, as if they have become boys again, nine or ten years old, but the stakes have changed.]

TOM GARRETT

We'll teach you a lesson, just like we taught Simpse. **(emphasis)** Fort Pillow. Whoooo. When we saw the colored fighting up against us...

ISRAEL

You keep Simpse out of this.

[Israel grabs at Garrett. Spotlight back to Cyrus.]

CYRUS

" . . . that whenever any form of government becomes

destructive of these ends, it is the right of the people to abolish it."

[Spotlight to Israel and Tom Garrett.]

TOM GARRETT
Anybody oughta know anytime you get hurt as bad as Simpse did that day.

ISRAEL
You keep this up. You're gonna need General Hood.

TOM GARRETT
They had to carry poor ol' Simpse off the field...
[Sings.]
"So now we're going to leave you, our hearts are full of woe
We're going back to Georgia, to see our Uncle Joe,
You may talk about your Beauregard, and sing of General Lee
But the gallant Hood of Texas played hell in Tennessee."

[Henry Garrett comes in.]

HENRY GARRETT
Hood? Hood! Ol' Fancy Pants!

[He grabs the bottle of wine from Tom and pitches it across the field, exits again, staggering. Patti and Simpse walk by again laughing.]

TOM GARRETT
"You may talk about your Beauregard and sing of General Lee, but the gallant Hood of Texas played hell in Tennessee."

ISRAEL

Oh yeh, well, I'll tell you what everybody in Tennessee
knows. When I looked in front of me, I saw white folks
runnin' like crazy, then I turned around--looked behind me,
never saw so many folks all crowded in, hills black as tar-
-the whole town of Nashville watching--your own folks. I
heard what the white folks said when they saw all you Rebs
gettin' chased by colored soldiers "nasty, stinking cows.
Why don't you fight? Look at 'em, just runnin away."

**[Tom Garrett backs away in anger, runs off the
field. Israel laughs as Garrett runs off. It is
growing dark. Children's voices can be heard.
Excitement is building for the anticipated
fireworks display. Major Daley enters and sits
with group. The tension heightens. Cyrus begins
to recite "Gray's Elegy."]**

CYRUS

"One morn I missed him on the customed hill
Along the heath . . .

[Eliza stops Cyrus and pulls at his coat.]

SIMPSE

Nashville, the Athens of the South, brings us a gift of
incomparable vocal artistry. Patti Bradshaw, a rare talent,
has traveled the railroads, South and North, from town to
town singing her melodies. Had Jenny Lind known of Miss
Bradshaw she would have retired at an early age. Miss
Bradshaw will favor us with a selection from Verdi's
Rigoletto. Miss Bradshaw.

**[Patti begins to sing _____. Shortly, Tom
Garrett returns. Garrett has a determined,
vengeful expression on his face. Comes face to**

face with Israel. Singing up and under.]

TOM GARRETT

One night I grabbed that gal Hennie, the one Brewer used to own.

[Israel turns away, laughs scornfully.]

ISRAEL

You sure took to talking ugly, right ugly, since you got back, didn't you?

[Simpse approaches]

TOM GARRETT

Maybe I turned myself into a Pa--just like you and Simpse gon do with that gal a his.

ISRAEL

Shut up, Garrett.

TOM GARRETT

I seen him **[to Simpse]** followin' her with his eyes. No tellin what else...

[Israel grabs Garrett by the coat and swings him around. Simpse rushes at Tom Garrett.]

SIMPSE

You say another word about Patti and I'll kill you right here and now.

[Israel pushes him back.]

ISRAEL

Say another word, Garrett, I'll finish you off myself. Mark

my words, you'll wish you were back on that hill.

TOM GARRETT

Mink Slide--that's the onliest hill you goin down. Only this
time...

[Patti begins to sing.]

**[Tom Garrett spins around. Grabs rifle and
points it at Israel. Yells out.]**

I got you now.

**[We hear rifle fire. The stage goes dark. We hear
voices of women screaming, children crying and
then fireworks, rich colors spiraling and
cascading in the darkness.]**

SCENE TWO

[Spotlight on Daley. Daley is pacing back and forth. Stage lights broaden to include Simpse and Cyrus.]

SIMPSE

Pa, it happened just like I said. Garrett takes his gun out. Israel grabs a hold of it. Tries to get it way from him. Gun goes off. **[makes sound]** That's all.

DALEY

That's all. That's all he says.

SIMPSE

Bullet grazed Garrett's head. That's all. Ol' Israel, he beat me to it. I was gonna grab Garrett's gun myself.

[Daley starts pacing again and mumbling to himself.]

SIMPSE

I saw it, Pa. Soon as Garrett's gun went off. He took off like a wounded polecat. Shoulda seen Tom Garrett and his boys hightail it outta there.

DALEY

Israel didn't aim his gun at Garrett?

SIMPSE

He mighta aimed it. Tried to scare Garrett off. Garrett was holding on to his own gun., Pa. Major Daley. Tom Garrett shot himself. And that's the truth!

[Cyrus sits in the corner with his head in his hands.]

86

SCENE THREE

[The next day. The Garretts are talking in a field on the Webster farm. Tom Garrett's forehead is bandaged.]

HENRY GARRETT

Always somethin' with you and Israel Webster, fighting all the time.

TOM GARRETT

Did you hear him, Pa? You hear him shoot off his gun at me?

HENRY GARRETT

Supposin' I did? You think I could go up against Cyrus Webster?

TOM GARRETT

Look at me, Pa. Israel Webster coulda killed me.

HENRY GARRETT

[shakes his head and turns away] You still here, ain't you?

TOM GARRETT

You heard him, said he was gonna kill me if we laid a hand on his womenfolk.

HENRY GARRETT

You ain't heard him before?

TOM GARRETT

Look at my hand, the way it's shakin', know why don't you?

HENRY GARRETT

Hush up now, look like death ridin' on a sody cracker.

TOM GARRETT

Pa, I'm your onliest son come back from the war.

HENRY GARRETT

All my kin went Union 'cept for you. All the way back to your great-grandpappy, Garretts never owned a slave. Damn you, it was Independence Day.

TOM GARRETT

Stars and bars, Lord, I love that flag. When I see it--Praise the Lord, I ache all over...more than for any girl.

HENRY GARRETT

What you say?

TOM GARRETT

I ache all over, Pa.

HENRY GARRETT

You goin' crazy. How you gon' git married, raise a family aching over a flag?

TOM GARRETT

Pa, listen to me, listen to me good. I ain't even had a son for you. What you gonna do if Israel Webster kills me off?

HENRY GARRETT

Kill you off? You and Webster? The two a you? Stop your whinin'.

TOM GARRETT

Pa, listen to me, I'm the one fought with Gen'ral Hood. I

can smell trouble a mile away.

                HENRY GARRETT
This war done drove you crazy, Tom Garrett. Hood? Ol'
Fancy Pants! You think you fought next to him?

                TOM GARRETT
Listen here, you talkin' 'bout the greatest soldier ever lived-
-General John B. Hood.

                HENRY GARRETT
Hood? That . . . you think he give a damn 'bout the
common folk?

                TOM GARRETT
Pa, look at me. You're smart, right smart...

                HENRY GARRETT
So they say.

                TOM GARRETT
You know how we live, don't you, Pa?

                HENRY GARRETT
 Live today same as yesterday.

                TOM GARRETT
Pa, don't you want a piece a ham every now and then?

                HENRY GARRETT
Ham? You got 'nough .

                TOM GARRETT
Pa, I 'm sicka dried up bread.

HENRY GARRETT
I work Cyrus Webster's land. You hear me?

TOM GARRETT
Soon as we put the scalawags in their place.

[Long pause.]

HENRY GARRETT
The Feds'll git you.

TOM GARRETT
They can't run this town forever. Ol' Cyrus see his son danglin', he'll hightail it outta here.

HENRY GARRETT
I tell you the Websters got friends.

TOM GARRETT
Cyrus Webster don't have no business with all this. Sooner or later we got to have that land.

HENRY GARRETT
You watch yourself.

TOM GARRETT
That land oughta be ours.

HENRY GARRETT
Cyrus Webster hear tell you after his land . . . me and Webster we got a good thing, you hear?

TOM GARRETT
Pa, I want a little piece 'a ham every now and then.

HENRY GARRETT

You do, do you? Fool! Don't you know Cyrus Webster got friends up high, folks wouldn't work next to you, save a sinkin' ship?

TOM GARRETT

Pa, can't you see what they got?

HENRY GARRETT

I see, I see Daley, Polk, Arnell, men own half this town.

TOM GARRETT

Pa . . .

HENRY GARRETT

"Pa ,we gotta stop 'em, Pa. we gotta stop em." Like Hood stopped 'em?

TOM GARRETT

I ain't playin' with you, Pa.

HENRY GARRETT

Don't you sass me, boy. Didn't you hear the folks yellin', callin' you names...

TOM GARRETT

I was in the mud, Pa, knee deep, but I'm home now. Look at it. Dry land.

[Henry Garrett looks around.]

The bright leaf, Pa look at it. Ain't it pretty?

HENRY GARRETT

It's pretty alright.

TOM GARRETT

[Tom Garrett goes to Henry Garrett.] Pa, we're on dry land now. Pa...

HENRY GARRETT

Go on from here.

[Tom Garrett refuses to move.]

I said move on.

[Tom Garrett clenches his fists and starts to scream. Henry Garrett pushes him out of the way.]

TOM GARRETT

Whole town knows what he did to me. Pa. Boys say they heard that shot all over town.

HENRY GARRETT

They ain't heard nothin'.

TOM GARRETT

Jethro did, called Frank, he called Lenroy, all the boys up at the courthouse, told them all about the Webster boy, they were pretty mad. Said I was crazy to let somethin' like that go by. Pa. he coulda killed me. **[unwraps bandage. takes his father's hand and brings it up to his forehead.]**

TOM GARRETT

L'il closer, Pa. Gimme your hand. **(takes his hand)** There. It's burning red. Ugly red. Here. Right here. Feel it. Skin flapping open. **(screams out)**

HENRY GARRETT

Israel Webster do that?

TOM GARRETT

He shot me Pa. Liketa tore my head open. Feel it again. Go on.

[Henry Garrett twirls around, gestures angrily.]

Me and the boys got our licks in. Ol' Israel ain't lookin' so good right now hisself.

HENRY GARRETT

Israel Webster... he did fight a white man...even if it was only you.

TOM GARRETT

They'll be laughin' all over town, poor old Henry Garret and his boy Tom let a darkie scare em, send em runnin'.

HENRY GARRETT

Matter of fact, he does it all the time.**[Beat]** You been messin' with the Klan?

TOM GARRETT

Lenroy and Frank, pretty mad, so they shoot a few rounds in the air--pass a few licks.

HENRY GARRETT

Boy, you wearin' me down. Stand still and listen. I asked you, you been talkin' to the Klan?

TOM GARRETT

I hear you, Pa, I hear you.

HENRY GARRETT

Well, stand still, damn you. Stand still.

[They stop and stare at each other. Henry

**Garrett pushes Tom Garrett to the
ground. Tom Garrett gets up slowly.]**

TOM GARRETT

No sooner'n I raise my rifle, doggone if the darkies don't
start firin at us. Israel Webster , you know he'd be in the
middle of it all. Much sense as he got, folks reckon he
planned the whole thing. [Beat] Say we git Webster?

HENRY GARRETT

The boy?

TOM GARRETT

Say we git Israel Webster, put him out of his misery,

HENRY GARRETT

I ain't said nothin' bout that.

TOM GARRETT

Ain't a jury in Tennessee let Webster go. Israel gon'
dangle sure nough.

HENRY GARRETT

Hold on right there.

TOM GARRETT

I can't go crawlin' back. Don't make me, Pa, don't make
me.

HENRY GARETT

Get this straight, they can lock the Webster boy up. That's
all. I don't want no blood on my hands, you here.

TOM GARRETT

I hear you, Pa. I hear you. **[Beat]** You all I got. One a these
days I'm gonna have a son, one name Henry Carl Garrett

II, spittin' image a you.

HENRY GARRETT

[laughs] That all you gon' have.

TOM GARRETT

Nope, I take that back , gon' have four or five.

HENRY GARRETT

Five?

TOM GARRETT

Feet turn in like so . . . every one spittin' image a you.

HENRY GARRETT

Fightin' and feudin' sunup to sundown . . . Alright, alright, damn you. You win.

SCENE FOUR

**[Cyrus is walking around with a pile of paper. He
picks up an object, examines it and makes a note
before going on to the next one. He hears a noise
at the window. In haste, he drops the papers on
the floor, gathers the papers, tries to hide them,
then moves quickly from the desk to blow out the
lamp. Hoping to surprise a possible intruder,
Cyrus hides in the dark behind the door. A
figure, barely visible, slowly enters and then stops
as if waiting for something. Cyrus freezes and
remains silent.]**

CYRUS

Israel, is that you? **[moves from behind the door]** Son . . .

**[Expectant. Still no answer. Cyrus rushes to the
other side of the room to a kerosene lamp. He
fumbles a minute. The figure, bent over, moves
closer to Cyrus. Cyrus raises lamp.]**

CYRUS

Israel? **[Grabs the figure and faces him directly.]** Lord
ha' mercy!

SIMPSE

If I'd wanted to, Pa . . . **[Simpse staggers in. He's been
drinking.]** It's a good thing old man Garrett didn't come
through the door.

CYRUS

Simpse . . . **[gestures as if to dismiss the comment, looks
Simpse up and down in an appraising way]**

SIMPSE
[imitating Garrett, using mocking tone, hands on hips]
Cyrus, your boy Israel's been cuttin' up out there. Cyrus . .
.

[Cyrus grabs Simpse's arm roughly.]

 We showed 'em yesterday, didn't we, Pa? You know,
before the war, they used to think darkies scared easy.
Show a darky fire, he'll buck and run.

CYRUS
[bends down to pick up paper from the floor] I've been
waiting here since dark.

[Simpse tries to look at the piece of paper.]

Never you mind about that.

SIMPSE
The bard working on his verses. **[Reaches out for a sheet
of paper. Cyrus pulls away.]**
I've written a few of those myself.

CYRUS
What took you so long?

SIMPSE
Rode all the way across town.

CYRUS
But you didn't see your brother.

SIMPSE
Israel? Ask Patti. She can tell you.

CYRUS

What was that?

SIMPSE

I said a man like Israel Webster, fought at Granny White
Pike, Battle of Franklin, all up around Nashville. He's a
fighter, Pa.

CYRUS

All the better for the Klan. Don't you know the word's out?
You think Garrett's the only one mad at your brother? The
Klan, why they're ridin' all over Maury County, won't stop
till they find him. Look at you. Not a care in the world.
Anybody try to come up on you?

SIMPSE

Pa, nobody's gonna hurt me. I lived through Fort Pillow.
Remember, I'm the one made it back, me, Simpse Webster.
Made it outta live. My leg's healed. My scar's drawn up
tight, smooth as glass. I'm strong, strong as an ox now.
Simpse Webster cured by the Almighty. Look at him. He's
grown.

CYRUS

You watch yourself, Simpse Webster.

SIMPSE

Shoulda seen Israel, woulda thought a cannon was aimin'
straight for Tom Garrett's head, the way Israel . . .

CYRUS

Boy, is that all you know?

SIMPSE

Garrett deserved it, that and more, if I could get a holda
him, I'd beat him . . .

CYRUS

That's enough.

SIMPSE

Give him bad dreams,

CYRUS

Simpse--

SIMPSE

The kind he had when he ran from all those colored
soldiers, cryin' like a baby.

CYRUS

I said, is that all you know?

SIMPSE

Yesterday, at the picnic, soon as I heard Garrett's gun go
off, I was with all of you, every minute, Pa, you, Ma, Patti,
the women and children, but it was crazy, you know I
could've sworn I was back there...back in the war. Pa, when
I came home, I couldn't believe I was still alive.
Everywhere around me, black bodies, boy's faces. **[touches
his face]** I still dream about it. They dyed the river red as
far as we could see, nothing but red everywhere, in front of
me, in back of me, no matter where I looked.

CYRUS

That's as far as you can see?

SIMPSE

I think about it all the time, Pa, them screaming "No
quarter, no quarter!"

CYRUS

Soldier boy, soldier boy.

SIMPSE

Pa, I still love fighting.

[Eliza enters.]

ELIZA

Leave it alone. Leave it alone, you hear me. Listen to me,
Simpse. I'm tired of it. Tired of all the fighting. And you
about to marry? Look at you.

[Simpse doesn't answer.]

CYRUS

Simpse, come spring , you got a nice young lady wants to
marry you. Don't throw it all away.

SIMPSE

Spring? Things happen so fast, Pa. When the fighting's all
around you, **[gets faraway look. We sense a feeling of
exhilaration.]** Pa, it's all you care about. It's your whole
life. Nothing else matters. I know this sounds crazy. Some
days I'd give anything to be back there. Don't worry. Of
course, I'll marry her in the spring.

ELIZA

What's got into you boy? I saw you out at that picnic. You
were about to kill any man even looked at Patti.

**[Door swings open. Simpse rushes to the door.
Patti stands in the doorway. Simpse walks to
Patti.]**

SIMPSE

Patti, I didn't know you were gone.

PATTI

Blow out the lamp.

CYRUS

Now girl, don't you worry, we'll let you know when it's
time to douse the lamp.

ELIZA

A girl your age out this time a night? You're bad as
Simpse.

PATTI

Oh, I'm used to being out. Traveling on the railroad, you
never know when you'll stop. **[beat]** Simpse? You been
out looking for your brother?

SIMPSE

That's right. Me and Israel. Just like the good ol' days.

**[Patti reaches out to Simpse. He moves away.
Goes and sits by himself.]**

PATTI

[to Simpse] I thought you heard me when I left the house.
About half-past seven I hurried in to a corner of the square,
to strike a bargain for a bolt of yard goods. **[She unrolls
part of a bolt of brightly colored fabric.]** I was in the
back of a store called Woolridge's, a few feet from a coal
shed out back. Not a soul knew who I was. Tom Garrett
and his boys, hidin away in that coal shed. They didn't pay
me a bit of attention. I could hear them laughing, Said the
darkies had no business having a picnic, that the law
shoulda run them outta there. Then they started in about
Israel, laughing, calling Israel a war hero, going on about
him trying to shoot white folks. Said the Klan was gonna
hunt Israel down. Tom Garrett--you should have seen him,
struttin' like a soldier, pretending to be Israel, marching
back and forth and yellin to his boys, that Israel was as

good as dead.

SIMPSE
A scout, that's what you need. If Tom Garrett comes this way,

[Patti cries out.]

I'll swing around Macedonia Hill, cut him off at the pass, I've done that plenty,

PATTI
Simpse, you can't—

SIMPSE
I'll make sure he stays away from the Websters. If ol' man Garrett tries to cuss me out, he'll hear the truth--for once in his life.

[Eliza moves in front of Simpse and stretches her arm in front of his body.]

PATTI
And get yourself killed. Come spring, Simpse, I'm looking to marry you.

SIMPSE
[Takes Patti's hand.]
I've taken care of men like Tom Garrett before.

PATTI
Simpse? **[dejected, then upright]** Didn't you hear me? I'm standing here talking to you. Flesh and blood, Simpse. I'm real. You don't even see me. Simpse. I'm here. Right in front of you. And, and you're looking right through me. **(yells)** Simpse Webster,

I'm talking to you.

SIMPSE

Patti, you don't…it's not what you think. I'll marry you.
(jittery)

PATTI

Oh, so you'll marry me. I see!

SIMPSE

There's something I have to take care of. Right now.

PATTI

And marrying me isn't worth talking about. If you don't
want me, Simpse, I'll leave.

**[Simpse and Patti face to face. Simpse turns
away.]**

ELIZA

Simpse, listen to her. You've got no business going out
there.

SIMPSE

Ma, you're looking at one of the best sharpshooters in
middle Tennessee. I said I was good. **[to Cyrus]** The way
youall talk, you'd think I'd never been to war.

**[Walks out, slams door, then walks back in.
Angered, Eliza moves in front of Simpse and
holds on to him. Patti stands behind her. Cyrus
goes to the window, opens the shutters, and stares
out into the night. When Simpse turns to go out
the door, Eliza blocks his path. Patti grasps
Simpse's arm tightly. A noise can be heard
outside, perhaps a tree hitting against the house.**

Cyrus walks over to the window. Stands there alone.]

CYRUS

Good, are you? You think you're good, but you just don't know.

[Patti sings _____ from _____. Her shadow appears on the wall. The shadow fades. The lights dim and then the lights go up.]

SCENE FIVE

[Eliza is at a table shelling black-eyed peas. As
she brings each handful up from the pan, she
works the peas gently, as if fingering rosary
beads. Patti is sitting beside her softly humming.
A parrot cries out from his cage. The door opens;
Israel comes running into the house. Israel rushes
in and embraces Eliza tightly, then hugs Patti for
a minute. Eliza abruptly grabs him by the arm
and motions him up the stairs. She sits down
again, pulls the pan closer and continues to work
the peas. Patti stands near the stairs. There is a
knock at the door. On the second level of the set,
upstairs, Israel slides in between the mattresses in
the feather bed. There is a second knock. Eliza
does not rise from her chair.]

ELIZA

Come in.
[She continues to shell the peas. When the door
opens, voices can be heard outside the house,
laughing and yelling. Daley and Garrett are at the
door. They stand by the door and address Eliza.]

DALEY

Howdy Liza, thought you'd be at that prayer meetin' over
to First Baptist. **(beat)** County magistrate. You know
somebody swears out a warrant, I have to see about it.

HENRY GARRETT

This here's official business. Got the law with me now.

DALEY

Henry Garrett's got something he wants to say. Garrett.

[Eliza nods. Garrett advances.]

HENRY GARRETT

[to Daley] Yes sir. **[to Eliza]** We come for your boy Israel.

[Patti stays near the stairs.]

PATTI

Ma'am, I'm sorry I meant to iron the bedclothes this morning. Slipped my mind.

HENRY GARRETT

Sure did show out at the Fourth a July picnic, didn't he? Sat 'pon my only child, aiming to take the poor boy's life.

PATTI

Ma'am, you want me to take that smoothin' iron to the bedclothes?

DALEY

Quite a little helper you have there, Liza. **[to Garrett]** She sings like a bird. **[points to Patti]** Reminds me of the voice of my dear departed mother.

[Patti goes upstairs and begins to arrange the bedclothes.]

HENRY GARRETT

Major Daley, sir. Sir, you hear tell Israel Webster aimed his rifle. Nearly blew my boy's brains out. **[to Eliza]** Where's your boy Israel?

ELIZA

Don't know.

HENRY GARRETT

You don't?

[Garrett and Daley start to walk up the stairs. Eliza rises and walks behind the men. Patti hovers over the bedclothes, smoothing and straightening them. Upstairs, Garrett opens a trunk and holds up a handful of tobacco, shakes his head in amazement. The two men huddle over the trunk.]

MAJOR DALEY

Cyrus Webster raises the best tobacco round these parts. Garrett, how many years you been working for the Websters?

HENRY GARRETT

Thirty next May, sir. Me and the Websters walk the fields sunup to dusk. **[beat]** No sirree. Not everybody can raise tobacco. Tobacco. Ain't it funny the way you catch the scent. Purty smell . . . we gone put a stop to all of it--your boy's backtalking, threatening. **[moves away from the trunk.]** Talking face to face. Looking a white man straight in the eye.

[Major Daley moves in front of Garrett]

Where's your boy?

ELIZA

[Eliza moves towards the bed.] Don't know.

HENRY GARRETT
You don't? You wouldn't lie to me, would you?

[Eliza turns away.]

A good Christian woman like you?

[Picks up Bible on table next to bed. Starts thumbing through it.]

MAJOR DALEY
Garrett, you lookin' for Israel Webster, you better get to it.

HENRY GARRETT
I ain't the only one either. They'll be out to get im. Woden't that him at the Fourth of July picnic, callin' decent folk names, claimin' white boys to be cowards in the eyes of the Lord?

ELIZA
My boy was raised in a Christian home.

PATTI
Ma'am, you want me to take that smoothin' iron to the bedclothes? There's a heap of wrinkles everywhere you look.

MAJOR DALEY
Quite a little helper you have there, Liza. Beautiful voice. Beautiful....
Liza Webster, honest as the day's long. Liza Webster, pray for a sinner, he'll never fall again.

HENRY GARRETT
[Runs his hands through the leaves. Eliza remains silent.] There's I don't know how many bags of tobacco

piled up round back. More'n you ever laid eyes on. Folks
long to have plenty tobacco. Crop to sell when things get
scarce. **(beat)** That's why they started up the Klan. There
was a time. A boy like yours would backtalk once, just
once. Next day he'd be gone. In the old days this woden't
happened. Your folks knew how to act.

**[Daley goes downstairs with Eliza. Patti
continues to fuss over the bed. Smoothing it
carefully.]**

DALEY
I've done all I can do, Liza. He'll be safer in jail than with
the Klan. Garrettt! **[Garrett comes downstairs. As he
leaves, he bangs his hand on the table. Bird cage
rattles.]**

HENRY GARRETT
What kind of bird you got there?

ELIZA
Ol' pol parrot. Used to have two.

**[Eliza sits down at the table and continues to sort
peas. Patti stands at the foot of the stairs. The
two men exit. When the door closes, Eliza shoves
the pan aside, spilling the beans onto the floor.
Patti rushes to her side. We hear the sound of the
bird chirping. Upstairs, Israel's foot slides slowly
out of the feather bed and dangles there.]**

Israel? Israel, come from up there.

SCENE SIX

[The sitting room of the Webster home, two days after the July Fourth. Eliza is putting away clothes.]

CYRUS

I was uptown talking to Major Daley, say "Cyrus Webster, you need to send your boy out of town."

[Eliza ignores Cyrus.]

Said I was uptown talkin' to Major Daley.

ELIZA

Maybe you ought to listen to the Major.

CYRUS

Listen to the Major? I'm way ahead of Major Charles Daley. Madam, you're talking to Israel Grant's son.

ELIZA

I should say.

CYRUS

You think I'd let them get my boy? You know how much I hate to see fighting. The only thing makes me mad is anybody laying a hand on you or the children. Maybe it's my own fear that makes me protect you so.

ELIZA

Protect me? Why Cyrus Webster! The Battle of Franklin --- I was washing in the yard--bedclothes... As long as I live I'll never forget....'long come a troop of Union soldiers, white and colored, come marching down the yard. Never heard such commotion, firing since daybreak. There I was standing at that big black wash pot, [Points] right out there. Glory be! A shot hit the side of the kettle, fell this close to my foot. The Lord was with me that day. A Yank, yaller hair, all in Union blue, come walking by, tipped his hat. And I kept right on scrubbing those bedclothes. Never batted an eye.

CYRUS

Now Dolly, I didn't know you were so fierce. Thought you hated fighting and carryin' on.

ELIZA

 Never said a word about fighting. That Yank coming by didn't scare me half as much as Israel's foot dangling out this bed [beat] Fifty years from now and we'll still be fightin' the war.

ISRAEL

[Israel enters, stands in doorway.] That's right. Ma--I didn't fight to crawl to Garrett or any man. Fought all over Franklin, Nashville. Fought like a man and I'm gonna live like one.

ELIZA

I thought you fought to be free.

ISRAEL

Where you been, Ma?

CYRUS

Israel
    [Israel bows head.]
You know who you're talking to?

ISRAEL

Remember, Pa, you're the one told me. I was already free,
free from the day I was born.

ELIZA

Free--you were, were you? Thinkin' every day they'd grab
you and sell you off. Hidin' Ed Daniel Calloway's family in
the cellar two winters in a row-- Me and your pa counting
all of you every night, the way you count sheep.[**looks
down**] You call that free? Son, didn't you fight to free all
your folks?

ISRAEL

Can't I have something on my own?

CYRUS

You do.

ELIZA

Your future's right here, son.

CYRUS

The only thing we have to give to you. I've fought this
battle for thirty years. I won't give up easy.

ISRAEL

Your land, your soil--walking the fields day after day. Pa,
can't you see it's fear?

CYRUS

Fear, Israel? That's wrong? First, I fear God Almighty and
after that . . .

ISRAEL

Pa, I'm a God-fearing man.

CYRUS

Then hold on.

ISRAEL

Hold on. "Hold on," he says. Independence Day. Get ready for a big time. They told me any man fought for the Union would never have another day of worry---all the protection Old Glory had to offer. Nobody gives you anything. Words, that's all they were.

CYRUS

Son, listen to me. **[goes over to his desk and picks up a pile of papers]** My will. It's all here.   This property, the farm, the house, everything in it.

ELIZA

Everything you see here.

CYRUS

It's for you and your brother.

ISRAEL

This farm? You think the black man owns anything? Tomorrow, they could come along, before you can say Jack Robinson, all of it gone, just like that.

CYRUS

Israel! You see this?   **[holds up sheets of paper]** Everything I have. It's yours.

ISRAEL

They don't care about that. **[grabs sheets of paper]** A piece of paper, Pa. Just like your speech out there...how many years now? Twenty-four? "We hold these truths to be self-evident"...words, [Tosses them on the table.] Words...You think a colored man's will means anything?

They'll laugh at you. Pa. Cyrus Webster, that ol' fool. All those pretty words and for what?

[Eliza motions to Israel.]

Pa...

[Cyrus turns away.]

Pa, I'm sorry. I didn't mean it.

CYRUS
The Lord says to fight the good fight . . .

[knocking at the door.]

Hold on!

ELIZA
Your pa'll make your arrangements, see you outta town.

ISRAEL
Leave you and Pa?

CYRUS
After things settle down you can come back.

ELIZA
Go on down there. You can hear when it's safe to come up.

ISRAEL
This is no way to live. **[hides in the corner]**

[A loud knock at the door again. Cyrus throws open the door.]

HENRY GARRETT
What must I do with these?

[Eliza stares at Garrett]

CYRUS
Come back after a while, I ain't got time for that now.

HENRY GARRETT
It's yours, what's left from our crop.

CYRUS
[busies himself.] I said not now. **[slams door on Garrett]**
Israel!

[Israel comes out of hiding.]

ELIZA
Maybe your Pa can talk to Mr. Arnell, some of the folks up
in Nashville. Son, we'll get you back home, when we can.

ISRAEL
Go away twice? Ma, if I leave this time, I'm never coming
back. **[starts upstairs, looking back as they talk.]**

CYRUS
Make haste now. You and your brother, don't go dawdling
up there.

**[Israel runs upstairs to Simpse. The two of them
talk back and forth for a few minutes. Patti is in
the next room sewing on a piece of fabric. Yard
goods are spread around her feet. Spotlight on
Israel and Simpse.]**

ISRAEL

What about Patti?

SIMPSE

What about her?

ISRAEL

You can't leave her.

SIMPSE

You think she wants me? I know what she wants.

ISRAEL

Stop all that talk.

SIMPSE

It's not talk.

ISRAEL

You're talking out of your head, boy. Patti's got too much sense for that. You think she'd give up a good life with you...

[Spotlight fades. Lights up downstairs with Cyrus and Eliza.]

ELIZA

We'll fix him up. Not a soul'll know it's him.

CYRUS

Israel Webster, there's not a man in town, white or colored, won't recognize that army imp.

ELIZA

You can always tell when his socks don't match.

CYRUS

That rascal--never did know how to cover anything up.

ELIZA

Makes every move in broad daylight.

CYRUS

No sir, can't change that boy.

ELIZA

No sir. Can't change one lick. Won't even try to.

CYRUS

What's that?

ELIZA

Won't try to. We'll send him off wearin' a dress and a hat.

CYRUS

A what?

ELIZA

A dress and a hat. I'll find something of Patti's.

CYRUS

My boy barely home from the war and his own ma paradin' him in crimson silk.

[Simpse comes running down the stairs.]

SIMPSE

Israel's leaving? Pa?

ELIZA

Don't question your father so.

SIMPSE

He'd never leave without me. Never. Me and Israel . . .

ELIZA

Simpse--

SIMPSE

It's all settled. Me and Israel are going North.

ELIZA

Heavenly father!
[Eliza starts to swoon.]

SIMPSE

You're talking to a seasoned traveler.

ELIZA

Where's my fan? Somebody get me my fan. I think I'm gon' pass out.

[Simpse runs over to the sideboard and grabs a fan. Fans Eliza.]

CYRUS

Get your Ma a glass of water, that feather pillow over there. Go on.

ELIZA

Never you mind a feather pillow.
[Grabs fan and continues to fan herself.]
Cyrus, will you talk to your son?

[Eliza runs up the stairs, starts rummaging through the drawers, opening and slamming them, crosses to look for Israel. Patti is at work in the next room. Spotlight on Eliza and Israel

arguing, then fadeout.]

[Lights up on Simpse and Cyrus are downstairs.]

CYRUS

Up North, huh?

SIMPSE

Pa, it's our plan.

CYRUS

Whose plan?

SIMPSE

Me and Israel's.

CYRUS

And stand on the corner begging?

SIMPSE

Not begging Pa, living.

CYRUS

No, I said begging. Who'll give a colored man a piece of
bread? Don't you know they'd just as soon knock you
down as look at you?

SIMPSE

Pa, you just don't understand. Me and Israel . . .

CYRUS

You and Israel.

SIMPSE

Me and Israel, we know all about the North.

CYRUS

You know what they say--a hard head makes a soft behind.

[Simpse looks off into the distance. It's as if he hears the music of the Sirens.]

And what about Patti?

SIMPSE

She'll be better off without me. You think she needs a man, roaming the countryside, coming back at Christmastime to see the children?

CYRUS

Just like that. You bring her here, tell her you'll marry her, one minute, next minute you're running off to the North.

SIMPSE

Besides I don't think Patti really wants me---not anymore.

CYRUS

Nonsense!

SIMPSE

Maybe she can come along but if she does---**[quietly]** Maybe Israel can look after her.

CYRUS

What?

SIMPSE

I said maybe Israel can look after her... Pa, I can't let my own brother down.

CYRUS

Up there you have to look back, but not for your brother. You have to check behind you, leave room in front of you, or they'll throw you out with the scraps from the kitchen.

[Eliza is on the stairs talking to Israel. She practically pushes Israel down the stairs. Simpse rushes to Israel and hugs him tightly.]

ISRAEL

A child like you? When did I ever say I was going anywhere with you?

SIMPSE

But we planned.

ISRAEL

I can't call my own name without adding somebody else's to it--Israel, Simpse . . .

SIMPSE

Simpse, Israel--

ISRAEL

Can't I have something on my own?

SIMPSE

.But we planned---

ISRAEL

That was me planning and you listening.

SIMPSE

Ever since I could remember we talked about it

ISRAEL

We did?

SIMPSE

How you and me . . .

[Israel moves away.]

The two of us. **[holds up two fingers]** Just like this...two on the same hand.

[Israel turns away. Simpse grabs him. Israel looks at Simpse. Eliza stands beside Israel.]

ISRAEL

That's enough, you hear.

SIMPSE

. . . even after the war. Fightin' side by side . . . Israel Webster, soldier man, shiny medals, yellow cord, your troops applaud you. Go on. That's fine. Make your own plans.

[Lights up. Knock on the door. Eliza hears knock at the door.

VOICE OF TOM GARRETT

Israel, you in there? We know you're there.

[Eliza goes to the door with Cyrus. Henry Garrett is standing there. We can hear voices outside. Sounds of rabble-rousing. Cyrus doesn't speak. Garrett walks in.]

HENRY GARRETT

Cyrus Webster, never meant for things to get like this.

[Cyrus is silent. Eliza stands off to the side.]
When Israel Webster called my boy a damn coward to his face, I had to set things right. The boy, he sassed a white man, even if it was only Tom; matter of fact, your boy, he

sasses all the time, has as long as I can remember.

[Cyrus stares intently at Garrett.]

VOICE OF TOM GARRETT
Come on out, Israel. The boys wanna meet you.

HENRY GARRETT
Now, you know, I never owned a slave. My Ma, she was a
Yankee: My kin, they all went Union 'cept for Tom. Well,
when I started talking to folks, other day outside the
courthouse,

[Cyrus raises his hand, then slams his fist down.]

. . . said I was crazy to let something like that go by.

VOICE OF TOM GARRETT
Come on. We got a surprise for you.

HENRY GARRETT
After the war and all I didn't think I'd see any grandchildren
but now... Allowin' Tom ain't been right-- since he come
back from the war. **[raises voice]** Talking face to face to a
white man. It's just plain wrong.

CYRUS
**[picks up chair, slams it against the wall, then turns
abruptly.]** So you come in here haulin' your crop,
'specting to get paid. Was that your boy firing on innocent
folk at the Fourth of July commemoration?

[Cyrus picks up chair, offers Garrett a seat.]
Sit a spell. Henry Garrett, was that you paid my wife a
visit, brought Major Daley along for company? Like to
scared the living daylights out the poor woman and that

young child Patti Ann? Your boy's been nothin' but trouble since the day he got back home.

HENRY GARRETT
Didn't mean for things to get . . .

[Cyrus paces the floor as Garrett talks.]

Honest, Cyrus Webster, I hated to see the Klan git into it. **[beat]** I want my boy back. Lord, give me my boy. Give him a decent place to settle down. I tell you he's gone crazy with this war. It's all he talks about. Like he eats and sleeps war. You hear me, I want my boy.

CYRUS
You and your boy, I want you outta here by morning. You get outta here right now, you hear me.

HENRY GARRETT
There'll be plenty to pay for this.

CYRUS
Your time's up, Garrett. **[raises voice**.] I want you off my land, Garrett... now!
        [Garrett pauses then leaves. Cyrus slams door]

ELIZA
[calls up and she goes up the stairs to Patti.] Patti! **[louder]** Patti!

[Israel enters room. Cyrus moves closer to Israel. Fadeout. Eliza upstairs with Patti. Patti sets aside her sewing.]

PATTI
Ma'am--

ELIZA

Israel's going travelling.

PATTI

These days you can go just about anywhere on the railroad.

ELIZA

Girl, he ain't going on the railroad.

PATTI

Yes ma'am.

ELIZA

We're looking to disguise him. That way no one will know.

PATTI

I thought Mr. Cyrus was against all that.

ELIZA

Girl, open your bag.
**[They open Patti's traveling bag, and she brings
out her Fourth of July outfit.]**

PATTI

My dress from the Fourth of July.

[They hold it up.]

I ran behind a tree, hid as many little ones as I could, the
skirt was covered with dirt. Washed it best I could.

ELIZA

[examines it carefully] One you wore? Uhuh. **[rejects it]**
Let me see. This one!

PATTI

[reaches for a dress on the bed] One I was sewing for
you, Ma'am.

> **[Eliza takes the dress.]**

You'd wear it well, Ma'm. Wouldn't you?

> **[Eliza and Patti descend the stairs. Eliza's hair is
> braided severely away from her face. She wears
> starkly plain clothes, a dark, floor-length dress of
> heavy cotton, a tiny row of buttons from the waist
> up to the neck, typical of the dress of matrons of
> that time. In her arms, she carries Patti's Fourth
> of July hat and the dress that Patti has made for
> her, as carefully as if she is carrying a child in her
> arms. Patti walks beside her.]**

SIMPSE

[reaches out to Patti] Patti---thought you were upstairs
resting.

PATTI

Oh, I've been up for quite awhile. **[turns to Israel]** Sewing
and mending . . .

CYRUS

Israel's getting ready for his trip.

PATTI

Oh the land around here--hills, now and then a valley--it's
awful nice, isn't it?

CYRUS

Nothing like it, nosiree.

ELIZA

There'll be a sack of beaten biscuits, a jar of peach
preserves. [hands Israel a small book]
Your father's book of verses.

SIMPSE

[points to book] Pa, this morning I saw Major Daley, said
you'd better decide on your inscription, said he had other
orders to fill.

CYRUS

[waves Simpse away] Took care of that long ago. You tell
Major Daley the decision's final.

ELIZA

[moves closer, carrying dress.] Your Pa's not about to
change his mind.

CYRUS

[to Israel] Before you know it, landsakes, there'll be the
grandest homecoming this town's ever seen. You'll march
home again.

[Eliza and Patti move closer to Israel.]

SIMPSE

[to Israel] When we left Peach Orchard Hill, I couldn't
believe we were still alive. But you pushed me out, made
me leave when I wanted to stay. I mean it was crazy, but
you know at first, I saw all those black faces and I thought I
belonged down there on the ground too. Then you called
out to me. I didn't hear you at first. Something kept pulling
me back, something wild. Just thinking about it . . . I mean,
I can't explain it, this sweet impulse, this sweet impulse to
stay there—with them.. Never saw you so mad--"Simpse,
I'm callin you, Simpse, you hear me?" I could hear you--at

first I tried to follow, but my legs, they felt so heavy, then
. . . something stronger.

CYRUS

Something stronger, pulled you up . . . both of you, pulled
you up and brought you back.

SIMPSE

I still dream about it . . . nothing but death everywhere. In
front of me, in back of me, no matter where I looked.
Before we left the hill, I looked down one more time, but I
saw things again, the way I hadn't seen them before. A
patch of flowers, ol' teacup blue . . . I could see it, feel it.
That little bit of life. No matter where I was, I knew then I'd
always find it--the way you will--in the rain, picking the
crop at harvest time . . .

**[The set darkens. Israel is sitting in a corner with
his face in his hands. Eliza holds his hand, then
embraces him tightly. Cyrus goes over to Patti.]**

CYRUS

Landsakes, that a new dress?

PATTI

Yessir.

CYRUS

[to Israel] Son, got my will ready. If the folks at the
courthouse order me to sign an " x," I'll get 'em straight.
Cyrus Webster's own pa taught him how to read and write,
hid 'im down in the cellar and taught him his lessons. That's
war. Sometimes you have to pull back before you advance.
Now douse the lamp.

SCENE SEVEN

**[The time is September, 1886. The sitting room of
the Webster home. Eliza Webster has just died.
Cyrus has preceded her in death by one year. If
we were to look outside, we would see that the
work day is about to end. The ground is littered
with crisp fall leaves, and the sky is tinted bright
orange and yellow, the color of a beautiful sunset.**

**Patti stands at a table in the sitting room. She
sings. As her singing fades away, Simpse enters
carrying Cyrus's jacket. Folds jacket carefully
and places it over the back of a chair.**

DALEY

[offstage] Simpse Webster?

> **[Simpse is fumbling with papers. Exasperated.
> Opens door. Daley enters carrying papers.]**

Simpse Webster? You in there?

SIMPSE

Major Daley.

DALEY:

I told your Pa…I don't know how many times…I knew…

> **[Simpse looks straight ahead at the major. Faces
> him. Holds handful of papers firmly.]**

SIMPSE

Afternoon, Major.
    [long pause]

DALEY

I told your Pa…that word…

SIMPSE

I don't think I quite understand.

DALEY

That word. You know the one. C-O-N-S-O . . . Going on twenty years and they're still talking about that monument….startin it up all over again. **(beat)** Here's your pa's will.

> **[Simpse looks over the papers. Daley starts to leave. Simpse goes to him and takes him by the arm. Leads him back.]**

SIMPSE

Major….Rest a spell. **[looks over papers, chuckles to himself]** In the name of God, Amen, I Cyrus Webster of the town of Delphi, in the County of Maury and State of Tennessee, being of sound mind and memory (blessed be Almighty God for the same) do make and publish this my last will and testament. After all my funeral expenses are paid, then I give and bequeath to Major Charles Daley, as payment for my head and foot stone, seventy five dollars and five pounds of tobacco. To my son Simpson Webster, a lot of land to be his property to have and to hold, and at his death, to become the common property of his children.

> **[Simpse and Patti draw closer to each other. He leafs through more papers. Shows one to Patti.]**

I give and bequeath to my son Simpse and his wife Patti Ann, the bureau, a large trunk of tobacco, one white counterpane, one small washpot, and a black fur hat.

[Lights dim slightly.]

"I further direct that as I am in possession of no information that would lead me to believe that my eldest son, Israel, is alive, he having gone North a long time ago, and no direct communication with him has been had for some time, that he Israel, be entitled to five hundred dollars from his younger brother, Simpson Webster, so named in this my last will and testament.

"I give and bequeath to Israel, in the event he returns, one trunk packed with tobacco, as full as it will hold on a damp day."

[Simpse turns to Daley. Looks directly at him. Long moment. Then motions to Patti, who is standing by the lamp.]

SIMPSE

Now douse the light.

THE END